SABOTAGE

SABOTAGE
ESKOM UNDER SIEGE

KYLE COWAN

PENGUIN BOOKS

Sabotage: Eskom Under Siege

Published by Penguin Books
an imprint of Penguin Random House South Africa (Pty) Ltd
Reg. No. 1953/000441/07
The Estuaries No. 4, Oxbow Crescent, Century Avenue, Century City, 7441
PO Box 1144, Cape Town, 8000, South Africa
www.penguinrandomhouse.co.za

First published 2022
Reprinted in 2022 and 2023

3 5 7 9 10 8 6 4

Publication © Penguin Random House 2022
Text © Kyle Cowan 2022

Cover images
Power station: © Willem – stock.adobe.com; Cyril Ramaphosa: © Waldo Swiegers/
Bloomberg via Getty Images; Matshela Koko: © Gallo Images/Sowetan/Esa Alexander;
André de Ruyter: © Sunday Times/Alaister Russell, Gallo Images/Business Day/
Freddy Mavunda; Sifiso Dabengwa: © Gallo Images/Business Day/Martin Rhodes;
Pravin Gordhan: © Waldo Swiegers/Bloomberg via Getty Images

All rights reserved. No part of this publication may be reproduced,
stored in a retrieval system or transmitted, in any form or by any means,
electronic, mechanical, photocopying, recording or otherwise,
without the prior written permission of the copyright owners.

PUBLISHER: Marlene Fryer
COMMISSIONING EDITOR: Marida Fitzpatrick
MANAGING EDITOR: Robert Plummer
EDITOR: Bronwen Maynier
PROOFREADER: Dane Wallace
COVER DESIGNER: Ryan Africa
INDEXER: Sanet le Roux

Set in 11.5 pt on 16.5 pt Adobe Garamond Pro

Printed by novus print, a division of Novus Holdings

ISBN 978 1 77639 059 5 (print)
ISBN 978 1 77639 060 1 (ePub)

Contents

Introduction 1
1. The more things change, the more they stay the same 13
2. The old hand returns 27
3. Rome burning 35
4. The report 49
5. The investigation 63
6. Further investigations 69
7. The new captain 83
8. The first battle 97
9. 'You're just bullshitting' 117
10. The second battle 127
11. The allegations of racism 141
12. Smelling a rat 149
13. 'We would like you to look after this place' 175
14. 'Did I mention the debt?' 185
    Epilogue 193

Acknowledgements 197
Abbreviations 199
Notes 201
Additional references 211
Index 213

Introduction

On an evening in mid-November 2021, as thunder rolled and lightning flashed, announcing a highveld thunderstorm, unknown saboteurs neatly cut eight steel supports – thick steel cables anchored in the ground – and toppled a small pylon in the veld near Lethabo Power Station.

Lethabo, situated just within the Free State border, some 10 kilometres south of the Gauteng town of Vereeniging, is widely considered one of Eskom's most reliable power stations, delivering power to the grid. Rated at 3 558 megawatts (MW), the six-unit coal-fed station is part of a fleet of 13 power stations that the state-owned power utility commissioned over many decades prior to the 2000s. Lethabo's first unit came online in 1985, and the last in the 1990s.

The pylon was indistinguishable from dozens of others in the vicinity, carrying power to and from the station. In comparison to the station itself, the 25-metre-high structure was but a small part of a large system of machines and networks that make up Lethabo's ecosystem. But the felled pylon was crucial; it supported power lines that fed electricity to Lethabo's kilometres-long overland coal conveyor, a critical part of the station's operations. Only someone familiar with the station would have known this.

It came down in a gravity-defying arc – falling up a small slope – and landed on top of another, smaller pylon that carried back-up power lines for the conveyors, instantly cutting off power and disabling the back-up supply line.

It was toppled just before 6 p.m., when demand for electricity starts increasing dramatically until about 10 p.m. This is known as the evening peak. Millions of South Africans arrive home from work and start cooking and bathing, driving electricity demand sharply upwards. Similarly, there is a morning peak from 5 a.m. to roughly 9 a.m., as people get ready for work and school. In winter, the peaks are higher.

Toppling the pylon at just before 6 p.m. almost certainly would have ensured that coal in the Lethabo bunkers would run out within hours, resulting in the entire power station being taken offline. And the loss of 3 558 MW on top of other breakdowns and planned maintenance that day almost certainly would have led Eskom to implement stage five or six load shedding.

'The perpetrators of this cut all eight stays. There is no sign of corrosion. No sign of metal fatigue. There was no shearing of these stays and there is clear evidence that there was some cutting instrument involved, whether that is a hacksaw or whether it is an angle grinder, that we will determine, but what further arouses suspicion that this was a deliberate act of sabotage, is that nothing was stolen from the site,' Eskom group chief executive officer André de Ruyter said with grim determination during a virtual media briefing on 19 November 2021.[1]

'So, the stays were cut, the tower was pushed over onto the other line, but nothing was stolen. So, this is not an economic crime, this was clearly now an act of sabotage and I think we can call it as such,' he said.

When the pylon fell, and the conveyor abruptly stopped, Lethabo had roughly six hours' worth of coal in its bunkers. It took Eskom distribution officials, praised by De Ruyter for their 'nimble footwork', nine hours to restore power to the conveyors, using another redundant line nearby. Fortunately, the coal in the bunkers saw the station through the evening peak.

'This would have caused us to lose our most reliable units at this point in time, the loss of about three gigawatts [3 000 MW] and would have put us into much worse than stage four load shedding, probably stage six load shedding, through a deliberate act of sabotage,' De Ruyter said.

'You will note that I am now calling this for what it is. For some time we have had suspicious incidents, but this is the clearest indication we have had to date that there are individuals out there who seek to really damage the economy by causing very significant and substantial load shedding,' he continued.

De Ruyter said the matter had been reported to the Directorate for Priority Crime Investigation, or the Hawks, who were assisting Eskom with the investigation. There has been little progress with the probe.

'At this stage we have no clear indication of who the potential perpetrators could be. It is of course immensely disappointing that there are people who deem it fit to intervene in our electricity supply, challenged as it is, in this particular way. But it's clear that these individuals have another agenda.'

When questioned on these details, he said that it was 'difficult to speculate' on the motive for the sabotage, admitting, 'It is something that I find very hard to believe but unfortunately, as I have just shown you, the evidence does appear to be at least prima facie incontrovertible that there is malice afoot and that we need to take action.'

In part, the revelation was vindication for De Ruyter, who had faced scepticism from the public over his ability to prevent load shedding, which early in his tenure he had somewhat rashly said would be halted. Instead, load shedding had never been worse than during 2020 and 2021.[2] Recovery efforts had been hampered by red tape and no less than the Covid-19 pandemic, which had the effect of drastically reducing electricity demand for months at a time, but that time could not always be used optimally.

When he took office in January 2020, De Ruyter became the eleventh chief executive of Eskom in six years – arguably the most startling indication of the turmoil that has gripped the utility for the better part of the past decade, as state capture and malice wrought incalculable damage to the company at the heart of the country's economy. Against significant odds, in January 2022, with two years under his belt, De Ruyter became the longest-serving Eskom CEO since the departure of Brian Dames in 2014, who spent four years in the top job.

Between 2007 and 2009, Jacob Maroga held the position. He was replaced by Mpho Makwana for a short stint before Dames took over. Maroga had succeeded Thulani Gcabashe, who had held the position from 2001 to 2007, himself having taken over from Allen Morgan, who was CEO between 1994 and early 2001. Prior to Morgan, Eskom was managed by Dr Ian McRae, who is today celebrated as a pioneer who oversaw the electrification of millions of homes in rural and township areas.

Nine men would occupy the office after Dames left and before De Ruyter was handed the baton: Collin Matjila, Tshediso Matona (who, perceived as a straight arrow, was unceremoniously booted from office after just five months, allegedly to make way for Gupta-friendly deployees), Zethembe Khoza, Brian Molefe, Matshela Koko, Molefe again, Johnny Dladla, Sean Maritz (who resigned before he could be disciplined for a questionable payment nearly made to a Chinese company ostensibly in exchange for a R1.5-billion loan), Phakamani Hadebe and Jabu Mabuza would all either be permanently appointed or act in the position while a new CEO was sought.

Many of those who came before De Ruyter will occupy the Eskom history books for reasons they would rather the country forget. Few of them will be remembered for bringing about any great revival of the utility's fortunes, despite vociferous claims to the contrary. So far, De Ruyter's tenure will be remembered for the worst load shedding ever – but also for the significant strides made in other areas, including a reduction in debt, better operating efficiency and cash flow with smaller losses, a massive corruption clean-up and, most striking, a series of targeted attacks on De Ruyter and chief operating officer (COO) Jan Oberholzer aimed at removing them from office.

The six years prior to De Ruyter's arrival are marked as the state capture years, during which, according to testimony by former board chairperson and acting CEO Jabu Mabuza, Eskom became the 'main theatre of state capture'. The corruption was perpetrated in the main by the Gupta family and their associates, aided and abetted by former president Jacob Zuma and his loyal cadre of compromised kleptocrats.[3] The tumult and treason of those years have been described by others in detail, including most recently the Judicial Commission of Inquiry into Allegations of State Capture, Corruption and Fraud in the Public Sector, better known as the Zondo Commission, which released its report in four volumes in the first four months of 2022.

Chief Justice Raymond Zondo released his report on Eskom at the end of March 2022, revealing that the state capture commission had calculated that a staggering R14.7 billion in contracts at Eskom were 'afflicted' by state capture, and recommending criminal charges against former CEO Brian Molefe, former CFO Anoj Singh and former acting CEO Matshela Koko, as well as the entire board of 2014. Former president Zuma and Koko, Zondo found, had been an integral component of the Guptas' capture of the power utility.

By February 2018, when Zuma finally stepped aside and Cyril Ramaphosa was inaugurated as president, there was already some reform at Eskom, with the appointment of a new board under the chairpersonship of Mabuza. Hadebe was first to be ushered into the trenches in early 2018, followed by a new minister of public enterprises, Pravin Gordhan. Their mission was simple – clean it up, fix it and save the country from the energy insecurity that manifested in the form of rotational power cuts, or load shedding.

But Hadebe resigned in mid-2019, citing health reasons. Mabuza himself would step aside in early 2020, effectively falling on his sword for Eskom's unkept promise that there would not be any load shedding the previous December. Professor Malegapuru Makgoba, a board member since early 2018, was given the nod to take over as chairperson.

It was into this maelstrom that De Ruyter stepped in January 2020.

He found an Eskom that was still shell-shocked. The utility was broken, demoralised and hollowed out, with ageing and brittle power stations that had been run too hard, for too long, causing spirits to plummet with every breakdown and renewed bout of power cuts. Furthermore, the continued load shedding was being used as a political stick with which to beat Gordhan and Ramaphosa whenever the opportune moment arose.

De Ruyter described some of the realities at Eskom as 'deliberate neglect'.[4]

The reasons why the system is so unstable today are relatively easy to understand, if harder to fix – for years, power stations were run too hard, sometimes out of necessity, but on other occasions because of bad policy and, apparently, the egos of past CEOs. Money was pumped into the major new build projects, Medupi, Kusile and Ingula, the costs for which ballooned from roughly R125 billion to more than R300 billion, resulting in desperately needed maintenance of existing infrastructure having to be deferred for years due to a lack of funds. All this means that Eskom operates at constant risk of load shedding. At any moment, major breakdowns, or an incident of sabotage such as what was seen at Lethabo, could plunge large swathes of the country into darkness for hours on end.

By all accounts, De Ruyter did not take time to settle in before kicking over a few hornets' nests. In fact, just four days into his tenure, he set in motion his first major battle that would nearly result in his departure. Eighteen months later, when poor performance was challenged in the key area of procurement, De Ruyter faced his second major battle, culminating in damaging but perhaps predictable allegations of racism. He was cleared, but the fight was acrimonious. Importantly, however, it revealed the hands of key players.

While there were positive steps in some areas, the continued presence of load shedding during De Ruyter's first two years meant that, very obviously, he was not winning the war. The Lethabo incident, however, clearly demonstrated that load shedding was not just a result of incompetence or a lack of expertise in Eskom's systems. De Ruyter could now show that he was also up against forces that were willing to take drastic steps to further sabotage electricity supplies – and him.

Clear evidence of sabotage meant that, in addition to the numerous efforts to destabilise De Ruyter and his team and the inherent instability of the fleet of power stations, they now also had to make provision for even less predictable and potentially far more damaging acts of deliberate damage that could happen at any moment.

How do you patrol hundreds of thousands of kilometres of power lines to ensure nothing similar happens again? How do you watch over the shoulders of every single Eskom employee and contractor to make sure that rocks are not being dumped into coal mills to occasion unpredicted repairs that would earn a contractor more money? And still manage a R410-billion debt and cash crisis, as well as hundreds of investigations into corruption to clean up the rot, and stave off orchestrated attacks in the boardroom and the media?

'I see this as my second *diensplig*,' De Ruyter told me during an interview in January 2022, referring to the mandatory military conscription of young South African men during the apartheid era, which was seen as a service to the country. It is easy to see why he feels this way: he and his team *are* at war. And the battle lines are not traditional; the other side are using guerrilla tactics and are apparently well versed in the dark art of destabilisation.

Critics argue that one felled pylon does not a campaign of sabotage make. But there are reasons other than Lethabo why De Ruyter believes sabotage at Eskom is a far more regular occurrence than is acknowledged. And he is supported in this view by other senior Eskom leaders.

According to COO Jan Oberholzer, Eskom received intelligence in late 2021 that a campaign targeted at 'creating havoc' would be undertaken in late January 2022.[5] Coupled with the incident at Lethabo, Eskom took this threat seriously and immediately deployed hundreds of security guards, intelligent CCTV cameras and drones equipped with infrared to all power stations, at considerable cost – as of 27 January 2022, the bill for this stood at R48 million 'and counting'.[6]

But the desired effect was achieved – down more than 9 000 MW of capacity due to unplanned breakdowns, including one of the 900 MW nuclear units at Koeberg and a 720 MW unit at Medupi, which had exploded in August 2021, there was no load shedding, and the expensive, diesel-guzzling open cycle gas turbines were not running.

Oberholzer came just short of calling it a miracle.

It was this intelligence, however, that confirmed in Oberholzer's mind that a campaign targeted at discrediting him, De Ruyter and by extension public enterprises minister Pravin Gordhan and President Cyril Ramaphosa was indeed under way, and that this campaign would involve sabotage of power stations. The fact that they had intervened and stepped up security only to have no load shedding was testament to this, he said.

Crucially, the incident in November 2021 was just one in a handful over the past three years that have garnered attention and intense speculation.

In June and July 2018, Eskom accused striking National Union of Mineworkers (NUM) members of vandalising equipment and of economic sabotage during strikes that the utility said had caused load shedding. NUM vociferously denied the assertions, but later agreed to demands from Eskom that officials known to have been involved in such acts face disciplinary action before a wage deal could be struck.[7]

In December 2019, Eskom was forced to implement stage six load shedding following several breakdowns amid incidents of suspected sabotage at Tutuka Power Station in Mpumalanga. Ramaphosa cut short a trip to Egypt to return home to handle the crisis. He announced that sabotage at Tutuka had played a role in escalating capacity constraints. Two thousand megawatts had been lost, he said, ostensibly because persons unknown had disconnected sensors that monitored the flame conditions inside the boilers.[8] The sensors ensured that operators did not continue to allow coal to be blown into the boiler after the flame had gone out. Thankfully, other protection systems kicked in, causing the units to trip.

According to one Eskom official, the president, together with deputy president David Mabuza, Gordhan and African National Congress (ANC) chairperson Gwede Mantashe, was briefed by a senior Eskom team shortly before the announcement. While the exact nature of the briefing remains unclear, it is understood that sabotage was explained as a possible cause of the Tutuka incidents. However, a year later, in December 2020, the National Prosecuting Authority declined to prosecute anyone, saying the evidence did not back up claims of sabotage.[9]

On 18 December 2019, thirteen days after the units at Tutuka tripped, a fire broke out on a coal conveyor at Majuba Power Station. Eskom confirmed to News24 that two valves controlling water supply to a fire-suppression system on the conveyor had been shut off some time prior to the fire starting. Eskom could find no record of a work order calling for the valves to be shut off. The conveyor was damaged beyond repair, and the structures carrying it had to be demolished and built again from scratch.[10] Meanwhile, coal was delivered to the power station by truck, at a conservative cost estimate of R150 million a year.

Oberholzer said that no one had ever been able to definitively rule out, or prove, sabotage in this case. But a project to upgrade and finalise the railway line leading to the power station was nearing completion, meaning fewer trucks would have been required to deliver coal to Majuba. The fire and consequent allegations against Oberholzer relating to the rail project, as well as an extensive delay in National Treasury responding to urgent requests for procurement-deviation approvals, ensured that roughly 1 200 trucks a day would be needed to deliver coal for a further three years.

In late 2021, Eskom finally commissioned the project and started taking train cars filled with coal to the station once more. By early 2022, Oberholzer said, it was expected that they would be able to ramp up deliveries by rail to eight train cars a day, reducing the number of trucks needed to 300 a day.

'But it's a 68-kilometre-long railway line,' he said.[11] The inference being that saboteurs could easily disrupt it at any point.

According to Eskom group executive for transmission Segomoco Scheppers, between 1 April 2021 and 27 January 2022, the utility recorded 2 752 incidents of vandalism causing an estimated R200 million in damage.¹² These incidents were not the only cases where sabotage was suspected, but with the constant breakdowns inherent in the older stations, it has become impossible to determine in some instances whether damage was done deliberately or whether poor workmanship was to blame.

In the third quarter of the 2021–22 financial year, Eskom recorded a 24 per cent increase in breakdowns immediately after outages for repairs were undertaken. Group executive of generation Phillip Dukashe said that while these outages amounted to just 1 per cent of the overall breakdown figures, they were still unacceptable, and Eskom had taken steps to investigate each incident and terminate contracts or discipline officials where necessary.

Intentional sabotage is not a new phenomenon at Eskom, although the motivation behind such acts has changed significantly over the past forty years. During the 1980s, when the ANC stepped up its efforts to destabilise the apartheid regime, there were many incidents of sabotage against strategic energy targets, which cost the utility hundreds of millions of rands. The most notable occurred in 1982, when four Soviet limpet mines were used to blow up large parts of the Koeberg nuclear power station, which was under construction at the time.

Years later it emerged that Rodney Wilkinson, a former South African national fencing champion, had planted the bombs that blew up in sequence on 18 and 19 December, causing R500 million in damages (roughly R10 billion today, accounting for inflation) and significantly delaying the commissioning of the power station.¹³

At the time, the armed wing of the ANC, Umkhonto we Sizwe, claimed credit for the Koeberg bombing and dedicated the victory to comrades killed in Lesotho just weeks before the explosions. It would take years for Wilkinson's identity to be made known.

The attack, arguably the most successful act of sabotage against the apartheid government by the ANC, struck fear and doubt into white South Africans. The pro-government newspaper *Die Transvaler* reported that, while the country was awake to threats, the Koeberg bombing and another attack where Sasol fuel supplies were destroyed suggested the government's preparedness was not at the level it should be.[14]

Wilkinson's actions were terrorism with a just cause, and he has been hailed by many as a hero. With the onset of democracy, Umkhonto operatives were absorbed into official security arms of the government. Wilkinson told *Daily Maverick* in a 2020 interview that he had spent years working for the National Intelligence Agency after 1994.[15]

Sabotage against Eskom as a tool of propaganda and pressure is therefore not unprecedented, and while the tools have changed, the sabotage at Eskom perpetrated in the past few years can undoubtedly be explained by a desire to see De Ruyter and his team axed amid an outcry over Eskom's failure to stop load shedding.

The worst acts of sabotage, however, have not been limited to physical damage to infrastructure – war is being waged on De Ruyter and his team on every front, from the halls of Parliament and the boardrooms of the utility's Megawatt Park head office to the dusty alleyways of far-flung power stations.

And these battles started well before the fateful November evening at Lethabo.

De Ruyter, Oberholzer and the new Eskom board led by Professor Makgoba have faced repeated calls for their heads, usually after seemingly orchestrated leaks intended to discredit them; have been maligned by certain media houses with half-baked conspiracy theories masquerading as journalism; and have faced multiple investigations into allegations of nepotism, corruption and racism. To date, all probes have cleared both De Ruyter and Oberholzer, but they have had to spend considerable time and resources fending off the attacks.

'The first 18 months have been unrelenting,' De Ruyter told me in early 2022, after his first break in nearly two years.[16]

Proving that there is a coordinated effort to unseat the current leadership of Eskom, however, is difficult. The conspicuous absence of the country's law enforcement and state security apparatus in probing the acts of alleged sabotage – both physical and reputational – is not a promising sign that they are enjoying any urgency. Instead, sweeping allegations against Eskom's most senior leaders have been left to play out in the public arena, forcing the utility to spend precious millions and time away from its core work to investigate.

In the past three years, the South African Police Service and the State Security Agency have remained silent, with the notable exception of Tutuka in 2019, which the National Prosecuting Authority later confirmed it had declined to prosecute. Little is known about that investigation and the subsequent decision made by the prosecutors. Now when the term 'sabotage' is uttered, critics point to the Tutuka incident as proof that De Ruyter is jumping at shadows.

Even when, during the media briefing in November 2021, he presented photographic evidence of sabotage at Lethabo, he was met with silence. While he confirmed that the Hawks were involved, law enforcement in general appears to be reluctant or unable to undertake investigations into the other serious attacks on Eskom's leadership, investigations that could not only solve a crisis for Eskom and the country, but also discourage others from making false allegations designed to distract and obstruct.

What greater threat to peace and security in South Africa exists than a collapsed power grid that would see millions plunged into darkness at once, the value of the rand decimated overnight and the economy destroyed? Perhaps a major terror attack, or a violent uprising stoked by elements loyal to the corrupt? The latter did happen, in July 2021, and there has been no urgency to investigate despite the deaths of more than 300 people.

Events at Eskom pose a clear and present danger that law enforcement does not have either the capacity or the appetite to fully address. Through it all, out of necessity and good governance, Eskom's leadership have tried to continue with a clean-up operation aimed at the corruption that has plagued the utility for more than a decade. Their efforts have earned them further vitriol and assaults.

They have waged this war mostly on their own. This is their story.

1

The more things change, the more they stay the same

It may come as a surprise to learn that the operational challenges Eskom faces at present are remarkably similar to the problems it had four decades ago – albeit on a larger scale today.

A capacity shortage leading to customers being asked to reduce electricity usage, rotational power cuts, a commission established to investigate the utility's affairs, allegations of corruption, cost overruns, unhappiness over increased tariffs, a bloated staff complement that had to be reduced, concerns over pollution, a major restructuring and sabotage all played out in the 1980s.[1]

The headlines from back then bear a striking similarity to what is written about the power utility today, so much so that they could easily pass as news reportage of current problems. 'Hit the brakes with power, Eskom might struggle to meet demand', *Beeld* announced on 19 February 1981. 'Evkom [or Escom as it was then known] has urged users to use less electricity during peak periods, especially in the coming winter months.'

The reason why Eskom was unable to supply enough power to meet demand in the winter of 1981 was due to a sustained period of economic growth that began in 1979, and which was projected to raise demand to an estimated 15 000 MW between May and September 1981.

A headline three years later, in November 1984, shouts about widespread criticism for Eskom's higher tariffs. In September 1985, another headline draws attention to the levels of pollution attributable to Eskom and its power stations in the highveld, with acid rain levels equalling what was seen in Europe at the time.

History at Eskom, it seems, is doomed to repeat itself – a worrying proposition in that, doubtless and without a viable immediate alternative, the survival of South Africa is intrinsically linked to the survival of Eskom.

The utility's biggest problem from a consumer and business point of view is load shedding. An increasingly irate public is becoming less and less willing to accept their apologies and explanations. Investor confidence is also being repeatedly shaken at a time when cash is desperately needed for renewable energy projects that may be South Africa's only path out of its energy crisis.

The capacity shortages Eskom now faces are the result of a perfect storm that has been brewing for decades – ageing power stations that were abused and run too hard for too long without the commensurate budget to undertake essential maintenance, corruption that has festered and spread, a two-year delay in signing agreements with independent power producers (IPPs) and, most importantly, a delay by government in giving the green light for new power stations to be built despite warnings from Eskom going back to the late 1990s.

To add to all this, Eskom is facing policy and regulatory challenges that are hampering its ability to right itself, with procurement leading the pack in slowing real gains. Eskom spends roughly R140 billion a year procuring goods and services – procurement that is governed by policies and regulations meant to achieve transformation, but which have failed due to corrupt individuals skimming off the top of critical contracts. Besides this corruption, a lack of policy integration and a failure to implement current policy are also causing major frustration.[2]

Procurement policies that prevent Eskom from doing the 'obvious thing' and establishing strategic, long-term relationships with manufacturers and suppliers often based in Europe or America are increasingly coming under fire from De Ruyter, who is advocating for a sea change and for policy to become more integrated, allowing greater leeway in procuring certain goods and services as he eyes better industrialisation for the country.

Arguably the greatest strategic blunder was the nearly four years it took the government of former president Thabo Mbeki to heed Eskom's warnings that the country needed to start building additional generation capacity. This was succinctly explained on 11 December 2007, during a fundraising dinner in Bloemfontein, when Mbeki apologised for power cuts that Eskom had been forced to implement.

'When Eskom said to the government: "We think we must invest more in terms of electricity generation", we said no, but all you will be doing is just to build excess capacity,' Mbeki said in comments broadcast on public radio, according to an AFP report. 'We said not now, later. We were wrong. Eskom was right. We were wrong.'[3]

Mbeki's comments were overshadowed by the political uproar caused just six days later when Jacob Zuma snatched victory and became the ruling party's president at the ANC's national elective conference in Polokwane. But his concession was historically significant for Eskom. As a result of the delay by government to recognise the need for major investment in the country's electricity infrastructure, Eskom was forced to act within truncated timelines to get projects up and running after finally getting the green light.

'During the early 2000s it was evident that new generation capacity was urgently required in order to meet the country's current demand, as well as to ensure adequate capacity to grow the economy,' Oberholzer, who worked at Eskom at the time, wrote in a June 2021 report. 'Government then, around 2004, instructed Eskom to build the much-needed capacity – needless to state that there was not sufficient time or resources available to effectively plan for the urgent capacity expansion.'[4]

The plan at the time was to spend R150 billion (R108 billion on new power stations) between April 2007 and December 2012 on increasing the existing generation capacity of 36 208 MW by a further 17 300 MW by 2020.

'The key generation expansion projects were the 4 764 MW Medupi and 4 800 MW Kusile coal-fired stations, and the Ingula pumped storage scheme in the Drakensberg, which would deliver 1 332 MW of hydroelectricity during peak demand periods,' Oberholzer explained in his report.

But there were several major problems with this plan.

'Eskom realised that it did not have the prerequisite skills and experience in order to successfully plan and execute these projects and would urgently need to acquire these critical resources. Very few of the human resources involved in the previous capacity expansion programme [which ended decades before] were still available,' his report read. Majuba, the last newly built power station in South Africa's electricity supply fleet, had been finished in the late 1990s and early 2000s.

The capital expansion programme, as it became known, included the building of two open cycle gas turbine stations, Gourikwa and Ankerlig. Completed in short time frames between 2006 and 2008, they brought online just over 2 000 MW of generation capacity for peak periods – but they rely on diesel and are expensive to run. In November 2021, Eskom spent just over R1 billion on diesel for its own and privately owned open cycle gas turbines to stave off worse levels of load shedding.[5]

The three other major projects – Medupi, Kusile and Ingula – were planned to be completed by 2015 and 2016, but the programme would face significant obstacles. The building of Medupi and Kusile was delayed for years due to design flaws, most likely the result of time constraints and, according to Oberholzer, corruption and a shortage of cash.

Costs also doubled. By late 2021, Medupi and Kusile would cost more than R300 billion to complete, according to estimates. Eskom had borrowed astronomical sums of money to pay for these and other key projects – the government had not only woken up late to the warnings over capacity constraints but had also then sailed Eskom down the river to find the money for the new power stations. The utility's resultant debt, hovering around R400 billion today, represents the single biggest threat to Eskom's financial viability. Most catastrophically, however, the programme resulted in the lion's share of Eskom's money being taken away from maintaining existing power stations, exacerbating the current crisis.

The reluctance of the Mbeki administration to immediately approve new power station builds was not due to concern over Eskom's ability to get the job done, however, but must be seen against the backdrop that, at the time, the utility presided over significant surplus capacity. In 2001, Eskom was named the best power company in the world and a shortage of generation capacity was, for those outside Eskom, a problem for the future.

Within six years, that reputation would come crashing down around the ANC-led government with the implementation of the first rotational power cuts, known as load shedding.

The events leading from Eskom's best years in the late 1990s and early 2000s to the first load shedding of democratic South Africa in 2007 and the marked capacity shortages today are defined by several important strategic decisions, beginning in the 1970s with large-scale investment in new power stations, including Koeberg.

With the sharp increase in economic growth in 1979/80, Eskom forecast that electricity demand would reach 16 300 MW and 17 500 MW in 1982 and 1983 respectively. Of course, demand today is significantly higher, peaking at 34 000 MW in 2019, due to the millions of additional homes in rural and township areas that were connected to the grid in the late 1990s and early 2000s, as well as a much larger industrial customer base.

By 1983, however, South Africans had become sufficiently fed up with Eskom's poor performance despite higher electricity tariffs that the government appointed Dr W.J. de Villiers to chair a commission of inquiry, which recommended sweeping financial and operational reforms. According to a 2006 paper by Dr Grové Steyn, incentives for managers linked to investment, particularly in major construction projects, had led Eskom to overly commit to building excessive new power stations. It was also determined that Eskom had overstated its future-demand forecasts.[6]

In the wake of the De Villiers' Commission, Eskom revised its forecasts. Some power stations that are today being run as hard as possible were mothballed, and construction on new build projects was deliberately slowed, although never completely abandoned. Construction on the Tutuka and Matimba power stations began in 1985 and 1988 respectively, and both were completed within five years. Work on the Lethabo and Kendal power stations commenced in 1980 and 1982 and took 10 and 11 years respectively to complete. Plans for a 4 000 MW power station that was to be named Lekwe were scrapped in 1986 because the government refused to stand behind the project financially.

Majuba Power Station, pivotal in the campaign against Jan Oberholzer in 2019 and 2020, was very nearly never built. Its last unit came online in 2001, with construction having started in 1983. Former Eskom official Sir Mick Davis reportedly viewed it as a 'big failure' on his part not to have got the Majuba project cancelled altogether prior to his departure from Eskom in 1994.[7] Eskom without Majuba's 3 800 MW capacity today is almost unimaginable.

By 2001, when the last of the new units came online, Eskom had effectively doubled the available generation capacity to just under 40 000 MW. Today this capacity is closer to 46 000 MW. Under normal circumstances, Eskom should be able to meet demand easily, but the full capacity is not always available, due to high levels of unreliability in the ageing and undermaintained stations.

There was a caveat to Eskom's increased capacity, however. Since the mid-1990s, the utility had undertaken a significant programme of increasing the number of homes that had access to the grid in a drive to electrify those previously excluded under the apartheid government. While capacity had increased, so had demand. As the new millennium dawned, Eskom made repeated entreaties to the government to begin building new power stations straight away. By not heeding these requests, the Mbeki administration made future capacity shortages inevitable.[8]

The early 2000s thus merely marked a period of calm before the storm as the country enjoyed reliable electricity supply thanks mostly to the visionary leadership of Dr Ian McRae, who had been appointed Eskom CEO in 1985 and had foreseen the need for additional capacity significantly earlier than his peers.

THE MORE THINGS CHANGE, THE MORE THEY STAY THE SAME

Current capacity constraints are not completely due to strategic decisions taken in the three decades leading up to 2004, but are also the result of slow-moving policy changes owing to political dogma that Eskom must be maintained as a strategic asset and a key jobs nexus. The millions of tons of coal that Eskom burns every year to produce roughly 90 per cent of the country's electricity and that contributes to ever-increasing levels of pollution is mined by hundreds of thousands of mineworkers. It is no secret that current mineral resources and energy minister Gwede Mantashe is supremely concerned about job losses in the coal industry linked to Eskom transitioning to renewable alternatives.

This was not unforeseen. In 2010, the government's own integrated resource plan (IRP) started the country down the road of cleaner, renewable energy sources, albeit belatedly. The establishment in 2010 of the IPP procurement programme was designed not only to provide space for greener projects (the only type of projects financing institutions will now pay for) but also to supplement Eskom's new build programme and make more electricity available.

It had become apparent that the new power stations on their own would not be enough. Ageing infrastructure meant that some older stations would have to be decommissioned, while environmental laws forced others to run at below optimal capacity in an attempt to reduce emissions. The answer was independent power producers. It was decided that renewable power projects would be awarded to private companies through a competitive bidding process that would be portioned into bid windows. Initially, the IPPs were criticised as being too expensive, but as the costs of renewable energy technology dropped, they were able to offer Eskom better prices.

The process stalled in 2015, however, when Eskom executives refused to sign any more power purchase agreements. In his 2017 annual report, acting group CEO Matshela Koko stated that the IPP agreements from bid window 3.5 (meant to be signed in 2015) were too expensive and a threat to Eskom's monopoly – this despite government policy, which determined that electricity had to come from diversified sources.

Koko bragged about his refusal to sign the agreements long after his departure. 'I refused to sign since June 2015,' he tweeted in 2018 when then CEO Phakamani Hadebe finally put pen to paper. He called the signing 'a big blunder', chiefly because of the expense. To bolster his argument, Koko claimed that, during his tenure, he had overseen a sustainable turnaround in performance and in the reliability of Eskom's power stations.

The arguments were met with scepticism. Yes, at the time IPPs were expensive, but then why was Eskom supporting plans to add more than 9 000 MW of nuclear power at an estimated cost of R1 trillion? Granted, nuclear power would be comparatively cheaper per unit eventually produced, but the capital costs and time to completion were risks the country could not afford. Soon after Ramaphosa assumed office, the nuclear deal was scrapped, but the electricity problems remained.[9]

And while Koko blames Eskom's current struggles to meet demand on incompetence, investigations by News24 in late 2021 found that a disciplinary card system that Koko had introduced for power station managers may have incentivised the running of power stations when they should have been shut down for repairs – adding to their increased unreliability today. It emerged that some station managers, fearful of being suspended without pay under the card system, had ignored significant faults for extended periods.

Koko dismissed the allegations as 'preposterous' and 'an attempt to undermine the best operational improvements of 2016, 2017 and 2018 under my leadership'.[10]

Koko has also made it a point to remind everyone that, during his tenure, there was no need to run the expensive open cycle gas turbines to stave off load shedding. While it is true that there was no load shedding during the Koko and Molefe eras between late 2015 and late 2017, what this really shows in my view is that other stations were being run into the ground in addition to new capacity from units at Medupi, Kusile and Ingula coming online and relieving some of the strain.

The result, News24 concluded, is that the older power stations are more unreliable and brittle today than they have been in the past, and in desperate need of major refurbishment. Nevertheless, Eskom is still running these stations very hard to meet demand. Load shedding in late 2021 was the result of units being taken offline for significant repairs just as unplanned breakdowns occurred, driving capacity down.

The renewed signing of IPP agreements and continuing bid windows is a strong indication that government recognises that Eskom will not be able to undertake new build projects in the time frames that the electricity is needed. In fact, another notable shift occurred in 2021 when Ramaphosa increased the allocation that consumers are allowed to self-generate without a licence to 100 MW, dramatically more than the 10 MW wanted by Mantashe and the previous allocation of just 1 MW.[11] What this means is that major companies with the resources available to them can now effectively build small generation units to self-supply and feed any excess electricity into the grid.

Various industries, including mining and particularly smelters, take up almost 50 per cent of Eskom's capacity and it is here where the economic effect of load shedding or load reduction – the step Eskom takes to reduce demand before load shedding is needed – has been felt the most. Yet the increase in embedded generation capacity was much to the chagrin of organised labour and hardliners in the ANC, who have stoked wild conspiracies that Eskom is being deliberately mismanaged to allow privatisation. The lunacy expressed by the unions and in some quarters of the ruling party is, at its core, contradictory and has rightfully gained little traction. It is the mark of a unique lack of critical thinking and realism over Eskom's position and prospects.

Very simply, South Africa does not have the astronomical sums of money needed to return existing power stations to a semblance of normality. Eskom, in the red for roughly R410 billion (down from more than R450 billion in 2018), cannot incur any more debt to fix them. And even if the debtor's book was lighter, international financing organisations are adamant that they won't continue to fund any new fossil-fuel projects.

In November 2021, Minerals Council South Africa CEO Roger Baxter called the increase of the self-generation allowance to 100 MW the government's biggest structural reform in two decades. At the same time, he announced that the mining sector was in various phases of planning for around 3 900 MW of renewable energy projects, up from a planned 1 600 MW the year before.[12] Over the past three years, Eskom's leadership has repeatedly expressed an urgent need for 4 000 to 6 000 MW of additional capacity to relieve pressure on the grid, which would allow them to undertake much-needed reliability maintenance and have a margin for unplanned breakdowns while still meeting peak demand – without the extensive use of pricey open cycle gas turbines. The question is why the embedded generation capacity was not increased much earlier. Government, it appears, has been desperate to maintain its monopoly on electricity generation – at considerable cost to the economy.

Capacity to deliver electricity reliably is not the only problem Eskom faced in the past that it is facing again today. The utility has long been a target for networks of extraction and patronage – in other words, corruption. The most memorable example from the 1980s is the story of Gert Rademeyer, a senior assistant accountant at Eskom who boarded a plane to Geneva in early December 1984.[13]

Hours earlier, he had convinced his superiors to pay more than $3 million (R8 million at the time) into his private Swiss bank account by warning them that an urgent business deal was at stake. The money, he told them, was to be a payment for the enrichment of uranium for fuel rods for South Africa's only nuclear power station, Koeberg. At the time, South Africa had refused to join international non-proliferation agreements. The company that was to be paid apparently did not have a bank account at the Bern-based Volksbank, so Rademeyer convinced his bosses to transfer the funds into his own account, and he would travel to Geneva to sort it out.

The transaction set in motion a series of events that would see Rademeyer convicted of fraud, and US congressional and federal investigators probing the use of Chase Manhattan Bank in New York by Eskom, which held an account there for 'strategic' purposes.

When he arrived in Geneva, Rademeyer transferred $500 000 to two accounts in Vienna, and a further $500 000 to a bank in Bangkok. He also paid $33 000 as advance rent for a 'posh' apartment in Monte Carlo. On 31 December 1984, Rademeyer returned to South Africa reportedly with a suitcase filled with 135 000 Swiss francs, which he deposited into an account belonging to his wife. On 4 January 1985, he left the country again, surfacing later that month in California, where he made phone calls to his lawyer in South Africa and to the *Sunday Express* newspaper. He alleged he was the victim of a cover-up of financial irregularities at Eskom, involving multimillion-rand deals that had been hushed up, and denied his guilt.[14]

By February, South African authorities had issued an arrest warrant and Rademeyer was picked up by Australian police in New South Wales. By July, he had been extradited to South Africa, where he stood trial and was later convicted, in September 1985, of fraud.

The Hollywood-esque story of Rademeyer's globetrotting exploits was major news at a time when stories of corruption at Eskom were few and far between. This is not to say that corruption was not happening. There can be no doubt that other significant incidents of corruption were commonplace, albeit less well known, in Eskom's past.

Fast-forward almost forty years and headlines about the graft that has beset Eskom in the past decade abound in reporting on the ailing utility. One example is the ongoing corruption trial involving former officials France Hlakudi and Abram Masango, who, together with the directors of major Eskom supplier Tubular Construction Projects, Antonio Trindade and Michael Lomas, and businessperson Hudson Kgomoeswana, have been charged in connection with a cash-for-contracts kickback scheme that will no doubt live in infamy.[15]

But their alleged transgression is nothing in comparison to the state capture mission of the politically connected Gupta family. So pervasive was their interference that senior executives, including CEOs, and board members who did their bidding were parachuted into the utility. By all accounts, the most infamous family in South Africa's recent history made off with billions of rands in looted money. But their efforts had another effect – honest, hard-working civil servants and professionals were driven out of the power utility when they refused to fall in line, robbing Eskom of institutional knowledge critical to its operations.

In an apparent effort to keep the critics at bay, power stations were apparently run ragged to avoid load shedding – the rotational power cuts nearly always drew attention to Eskom's operational matters and had to be avoided while the looting was perpetrated.

Nevertheless, investigative journalists aided by whistleblowers were able to piece together the dodgy coal deals and machinations under way. Thuli Madonsela, the Public Protector at the time, was even more successful, but the end of her term of office hampered her efforts to continue investigating. Her October 2016 'State of Capture' report was, however, enough. She recommended that a judicial commission of inquiry be established to get to the bottom of it all – and the Zondo Commission was born.

Testimony before the commission was jaw-dropping and disheartening. The more than 400 days of oral evidence uncovered just how deep the state capture project ran – and how close South Africa had come to a sort of corporate coup d'état.

It was against this backdrop that, in early 2018, President Cyril Ramaphosa took several important steps. Firstly, he appointed a new Eskom board and asked Jabu Mabuza to steer the ship – this was achieved while Zuma was still in office in January 2018. He also appointed Phakamani Hadebe as acting CEO, an appointment that would be made permanent in May. And, shortly after being sworn in as president in February, he made Pravin Gordhan his minister of public enterprises.

Secondly, that April, Ramaphosa signed a Special Investigating Unit (SIU) proclamation that mandated the SIU to undertake sweeping investigations into Eskom's affairs well beyond the terms of reference of the Zondo Commission.

The following month, Gordhan held a media briefing on state-owned enterprises (SOEs), in which he announced changes to various boards and revealed the broad strokes of his mandate to these boards: clean up the past, investigate what needs to be investigated, pursue charges if necessary and clear out people who are toxic.

The SIU and Eskom did not delay. Eskom appointed Bowmans law firm, which has a formidable forensic investigation division, to help investigate large parts of the utility's affairs, including the new build programmes and the accompanying multibillion-rand contracts.

By July 2018, Eskom had appointed Jan Oberholzer as COO. A highly experienced former Eskom official, Oberholzer had the operational know-how to steer the utility out of the doldrums. Within days of taking up the position, Oberholzer signed a mandate authorising Bowmans to start investigating several key contracts at Kusile, the beleaguered and delayed new power station being built in Mpumalanga. Kusile, one of Eskom's biggest projects since democracy, had become a cesspool of corruption that had been allowed to run almost unchecked.

It is thanks to Bowmans that Eskom has had some success in probing a R100-million kickback scheme involving senior Eskom officials and numerous multinationals and JSE-listed companies. As already mentioned, one set of transactions has ended up in court, with charges of fraud and corruption chief among a laundry list of allegations against former Eskom officials Hlakudi and Masango, who are in the dock alongside Tubular Construction Projects' Trindade and Lomas, who is facing extradition from the UK with a trial date set for early May 2022, and apparent businessperson Kgomoeswana and his company Babinatlou Business Services.[16]

Several construction companies, including Tubular, Esor Construction, Tenova Mining & Minerals and Stefanutti Stocks, paid a combined R100 million to Babinatlou, which prosecutors allege was for the benefit of Hlakudi, Masango and several other Eskom officials. Esor, Tenova and Stefanutti Stocks are yet to face prosecutors in court, however, despite investigations being either complete or close to finalisation. Bowmans' work was crucial to securing the evidence that shows how the Eskom employees allegedly manipulated claims and contract-modification processes to benefit the companies that have been paid billions for work on Kusile.

So far this is the only case before court. While some of the delays in bringing the other companies to book can be explained, one case involving a former senior Eskom official has languished on prosecutors' desks for at least three years.

In May 2021, News24's investigative team published the first in a series of exposés based on a trove of leaked documents, including thousands of pages of letters, forensic reports, emails, bank statements and payment analyses. Dubbed the 'Eskom Files' and provided to News24 and the Global Initiative against Transnational Organized Crime, the documents revealed the depth and breadth of corruption at Eskom, the extent and current state of the investigations into the graft, and, more alarmingly, the extensive efforts from inside Eskom to discredit and sabotage the various probes by law enforcement agencies and private firms, including the deliberate scuppering of investigations that had secured the return of nearly R2 billion.

The Eskom Files showed that everything from the multibillion-rand contracts for securing the country's electricity supply to the contracts for knee guards, mops, and tea, milk and sugar for the head office in Woodmead had been tainted by corruption and irregularities. Eskom was in a desperate state and required immediate, life-saving interventions.

Chief among the priorities was to investigate and prosecute major instances of corruption, which would not only signal that change was coming but also clear out the nefarious elements working against Eskom's best interests. The utility therefore needed steady hands, leaders who would not bow to political pressure or interference, and who would steer Eskom away from the brink of disaster wrought by the machinations of state capture and a decade of mismanagement. It was a task that would be far more difficult than anyone could have imagined.

2

The old hand returns

Eskom has been part of Jan Oberholzer's life in one way or another for more than 50 years.

When he returned to the power utility in July 2018 as its COO, he had been in the private sector for a decade after working at Eskom for 26 years between 1983 and December 2008. Before he joined the utility as a trainee engineer in 1982, his father had already worked at Eskom for more than two decades. Jacobus Oberholzer was a linesman and worked for 23 years installing rural reticulation lines. He would die, in 1981, aged 60, just two years after he became a supervisor and was given his own team of linesmen to oversee.

As fate would have it, 14 years later, Oberholzer, who from 1995 was appointed to manage Eskom's massive electrification programme, which brought power to millions of homes in areas that had previously been excluded from the national grid, would from time to time find himself working on lines that his father had helped build.

He has a picture of his father in his office at Eskom.

'There were quite a few of the lines he and his team had built, and that was quite an experience. At the time he had already passed,' Oberholzer told me.[1]

He was born on 26 April 1958 in Springs, at Far East Rand Hospital where his mother, Anna, who died in August 2021 aged 90, worked as a nurse and which was also incidentally where she met Jacobus after he had an accident and had to be taken to the hospital for treatment. While Oberholzer and his sister were still young, the family relocated to

Emalahleni, or Witbank as it was then known, where their father got his first job at Eskom.

'I sort of grew up in an Eskom house, since I could understand and got my brains – if you talk to my wife, she will tell you that I got my brains quite late – but ever since I could remember, my dad worked for Eskom,' he laughed. 'It was just a normal, middle-class home in which I grew up, with lots of love. Once a year we went on holiday to St Lucia, my father was mad about fishing, with our caravan.'

Oberholzer attended Witbank Technical High School and, from 1976, after his father had obtained an Eskom bursary for his son for his years of service, the University of Pretoria (UP), where he would take a little longer than most to complete a degree in electrical engineering.

'You must understand, I had to play rugby,' he said slyly, wagging a finger.

At the time, South Africa still presided over a conscription system, and young men who did not immediately attend university after finishing high school had to complete two years of national service. Those who did study had to complete national service after obtaining their degree. Oberholzer would end up in the navy.

'When I graduated, you know, one tends to be very idiotic, stupid. When I graduated, I wrote the defence force a letter and told them about this very brilliant young engineer. At the time they had called me up to, I think 4 SAI [South African Infantry Battalion] and 7 SAI, which was motorised infantry and I told them, no man, I am this brilliant guy, I want to join the air force and if the air force don't take me, it's actually going to be a helluva loss to them,' Oberholzer said. 'So I suppose this guy read my letter and said, where can I send this guy, as far as possible? So they sent me to Saldanha Bay! When I got the letter I couldn't believe it, I didn't even know where Saldanha was. But that's how I ended up in the navy. All I can think is that this guy got such a *knak* in me after reading my letter, and thought, you know, where can I send this guy?' Oberholzer laughed as he recounted the tale. 'But I never regretted it.'

THE OLD HAND RETURNS

After completing basic training in Saldanha Bay, a small port town on the West Coast, he completed his officer's course in Gordon's Bay and spent the last 19 months of his national service in the navy dockyard in Durban.

'I did quite a lot of engineering projects for the dockyard, so I was very blessed. I can remember that I got a letter from the admiral of the navy at the time thanking me for my contribution.'

The projects included assisting in the designs of a DC power supply for a synchro lift – used to lift ships out of the sea – and a high-powered lighting system for the sports field, and drafting operating regulations for work on high-voltage power lines for the navy.

'I enjoyed the two years, even if I didn't look forward to it. Being a graduate engineer, you want to start making a contribution. Then you have to take two years out of your life, but that is where I learned additional discipline, and what it means to serve your country.'

Immediately prior to his national service, Oberholzer had done a six-month stint as a trainee engineer at Eskom's Duvha Power Station and national control, where he was given hands-on training. Eskom bursars, he explained, had to work for the utility for two years after completing their studies. After national service, he returned to Eskom where he would remain for more than two decades. It was during a short holiday between graduation and taking up his work at Eskom that Oberholzer met his wife, Lindy.

He had returned to St Lucia for some fishing and to unwind with a close friend, Chris van der Walt, when, one afternoon, they noticed a family – husband and wife with two daughters and a son – struggling to navigate the St Lucia sand dunes with a caravan in tow. Being considerably experienced in such delicate operations, learned over many years attending the same area for holidays as a child, Oberholzer and his friend sprang into action.

Lindy was the eldest daughter. Despite a flooded tent doubtless due to a slight miscalculation in the placement of the caravan, a few years later they would be married. Oberholzer admitted that some fishing did in fact take place. While he still cherishes a deep love for fly fishing, he rarely has time nowadays, devoting his days and most weekends to Eskom.

Shortly after tying the knot in early 1986, Oberholzer was appointed as a district manager for Sabie for six months before being transferred to Lydenburg, a small town in the Mpumalanga highveld, where he took on the role of Eskom manager for around 2 500 customers.

'It was a stunning time in my life – you were close to the customer, it was one-stop service, you know. Granted the technology wasn't as advanced as it is today, but there was that personal contact with the customer. I can remember one day there was somebody who was very upset, and he wanted to come and address me. Fortunately, my secretary at the time, Alida du Preez, managed to calm him down with some coffee and so on, and afterward this farmer and I became quite good friends,' Oberholzer laughed. 'But that personal touch has disappeared, that thing where, if a customer is unhappy, he can get in his car and come and see Eskom and talk to them.'

After three years in Lydenburg, Oberholzer relocated to Nelspruit, where he was later appointed regional manager. In 1992, he was moved to Pretoria to manage the capital expansion programme for distribution. In 1995, he was appointed to oversee one of the largest electrification programmes in the world. South Africa, a newly democratic country at that stage, had to address the historical exclusion from the grid of millions of homes, based largely on racist policies introduced by previous governments before and during apartheid. Within two years, Oberholzer had to meet a target of 300 000 homes annually.

In the early days, there was no nationally coordinated strategy or plan to undertake this mammoth task, he explained.

'When we started off, we gave everyone a Rolls-Royce, because we didn't know any better, and we did it the traditional way, three open wires and a transformer. There was no optimisation,' Oberholzer recalled. 'This is why we then tackled it as an integrated approach. I mean, when you talk about electrification, it sounds so easy. But how do you get all the poles, all the conductors, the transformers? Where do you get the contractors, the consultants? We put together a wholistic, integrated programme, and it took us some time.'

Oberholzer credits the technical manager of the programme, Rob Stephen, who retired from Eskom in 2020, as being instrumental in ensuring the designs of the systems were adequate. Over four years, Oberholzer and his team managed to achieve a cost reduction of more than 30 per cent, simply because he refused to pay more.

'We had lots of engagements, I personally, with suppliers, and I said to them, and shared with them, this is the programme, this is what we want from you, this is the volumes we need. But please know, if we give you all this, you *will* give us a better price. I had lots of fights with the suppliers, a lot of them I suppose still hate me because I took a lot of profit away from their companies. It was the same with the contractors and the consultants.'

Three years into the programme, Oberholzer had to tell the team to slow down, as they were connecting too many homes and Eskom didn't have the money to pay suppliers for more than 300 000 a year.

'What was incredible, everybody that worked on the electrification, the whole team, they saw, they realised and they took accountability for the importance of the electrification,' Oberholzer said.

He related how, a few years before returning to Eskom, he was called by one of the former contractors, offering him a job in Dubai.

'But why, I asked? He said they needed somebody who can tell people where to get off! That was the way I was. Mind you, that's how I still am,' he chuckled. 'And if I look back now, and this is what for me is very sad, that was a massive programme, and never ever did any corruption get to my table. It was not to enrich ourselves, but it was about how do we make a positive contribution to the people of South Africa that never had access to electricity?'

It was in one such village, near Groblersdal, where Oberholzer said he found his purpose in life. One late afternoon, they were due to switch on the power to the village and a village elder was chosen to flip the switch.

'That was really just a switch, we had the walkie-talkie to tell the guy to switch on the breaker. And the whole village had gathered, they were standing there, all the wives and children and we had a little bit of a speech and suddenly it was time for the village chief to switch on the lights,' he recalled. 'And all of a sudden the lights came on. The joy that I experienced looking at the people's faces when, for the first time in their lives, they had access to electricity. There I realised my purpose in life, to make a positive contribution to the lives of others. I had to turn nearly 40 years old to really understand my life's purpose. Then we started with the big build programme, Medupi and Kusile, and it was about how much can be stolen. Really, it's sad.'

Oberholzer wakes every morning at around 3 a.m. and then has a cup, or three, of strong coffee while he has quiet time, which he uses to reflect and pray.

'Not later than four, usually around half past three, I start my admin, until about quarter past five when I leave for work. This has been most of my life. If you are not prepared to work hard, you cannot expect to reap benefits. There is a portion of luck as well, but I believe, and this is what I taught my boys, if you work hard, your opportunities will come. And it's not about you, yes in a way it is, you need some money to enjoy what you are doing, but you are here because God put you here, so you have a purpose in life, and understanding what that purpose is while having fun, enjoying what you are doing.'

He and Lindy have three sons – Jacques, the eldest who is autistic, Francois and Armand. Having an autistic child was a uniquely painful and difficult experience, he said, particularly for Lindy.

'When we identified that Jacques was autistic, we took him to a medical doctor, and I won't mention his name, this person, this doctor, let me be professional today, then informed Lindy that Jacques is autistic, we must understand that he is going to be a vegetable, and that we need to put him in a home, and love him and leave him there,' Oberholzer told me, with a note of anger.

Jacques, who still lives with his parents, drives his own car to work at a company that builds wooden shop fittings, and drives himself home.

'This because of the time and the energy, discipline, love, whatever you want to call it, my wife gave this boy, this son of ours. It was an extremely, extremely difficult road. But what he is today, is because of his mom. She sort of counsels a lot of parents that had similar challenges. And what we find, and what she tells them, it's not a once-off, it's going to be a long process, and it's going to be painful. What she has done, in my view, is just a flippen miracle, it's incredible.'

Thirty years ago, when Jacques was born, little was known or understood about autism. At a wedding one day, Oberholzer and his wife were chatting to a professor from the University of Johannesburg, who told Lindy that a dissertation on what she had been able to achieve with her son would easily earn her a master's degree. She started, Oberholzer said, but stopped.

'And I said, but you will have a master's degree! And she said, "It's not about the degree, it's too painful for me to write down." Jacques is an incredible human being today. I have to give all the credit, obviously to God, but to Lindy as well.'

Their middle son, Francois, has a degree in geology and environmental management, while the youngest, Armand, is an electrical engineer who graduated in 2021. Both studied at the University of Potchefstroom. Oberholzer laughed when asked if either of them will follow in his footsteps and work for Eskom. It's unlikely, he said, but it would have been nice to have a third generation work at the utility.

'Take where I am coming from – my dad worked for Eskom for 25 years. At the time, his brother worked for Eskom. His cousins worked for Eskom, my brother-in-law, my sister's husband, worked for Eskom. My sister worked a little bit for Eskom. What we are today as the Oberholzer family is because of Eskom. We gave our side, but Eskom gave us the opportunity.'

In July 2023, a few months after he turns 65, and assuming Oberholzer is still at the power utility, he will have a combined 30 years' service, with the most recent years as COO.

I asked him whether he considered Eskom to be deeply part of his life.

'Oh yes,' he said.

Between early 2000 and 2004, after overseeing the electrification programme, he was appointed to a senior position at Technology Services International, an Eskom subsidiary responsible for research, testing and development.

'At the time, Eskom decided let's go and conquer the world, let's go and show everybody how good we are. I was part of Eskom Enterprises, and the thinking was let's go and get businesses all over the show. I was very privileged to work in Libya … and Mali, in the Philippines. That was a time that we really wanted to go into Africa and the world and build, create some businesses. At the time we also got this concession which we still have, in Uganda.

'Meanwhile, Rome was starting to burn back home,' Oberholzer said.

3

Rome burning

TEN YEARS BEFORE HE RETURNED to Eskom, Oberholzer had been deeply involved in conceptualising and putting in place the major new build projects that were meant to solve South Africa's electricity stranglehold.

He had left Technology Services International in 2004 and joined Peter O'Connor, a vastly experienced Eskom manager, to establish what is today known as the group capital division. There were major problems ahead, and Eskom had seen the writing on the wall.

'Back in the late 1990s, we alerted government that we were going to run out of power in the middle 2000s, around 2005 to 2008. We said, we are going to run out of power if we don't build new power stations,' Oberholzer told me. 'I never saw the letters or whatever from government, but I was in meetings where we discussed, where government gave us feedback, you know, please note Eskom, stay in your lane. New power stations will be built by independent power producers – that's what we were told.'[1]

For years, government maintained this line.

'I can recall, I think it was the 24th of November 2004, the chief exec at the time, Thulani Gcabashe, walked into my office and said, Jan, now we are really going to get going. I said, what's it, Thulani? And he said, you are going to build two open cycle gas turbines.'

These turned out to be Ankerlig and Gourikwa.

'You are trying to get ready for this new build, it's again the same as at the time of electrification, you know things are coming, but you don't know what is actually coming or what you need to do. Two years later, we had both power stations up and running.'

While construction on the two open cycle gas turbines was under way, Eskom realised 'we were in serious, serious problems', Oberholzer said. They had to build new capacity urgently, and Medupi and Kusile – Projects Alpha and Bravo at the time – were born.

'I can remember when, in 2006, we went to Medupi, next to Matimba in Limpopo, and all you could see were trees, there was nothing, and we said this is where the power station is going to be. At the time I was so stupid, I said, right, let's get going, let's get the bulldozers. But a guy said, uh-huh, what about the trees? What about this, what about that? So, it was quite fun. We had to get a nursery, because whatever you take out, later you have to put it back!'

A year later, he recalled standing next to the N4 highway at Balmoral in Mpumalanga, observing a completely different landscape and looking at the site where Kusile would be built. But, as Oberholzer related, Rome was already burning. The megalithic coal stations and Ingula in KwaZulu-Natal, a pumped storage scheme that would be used during peak periods, had been started too late.

Together, the three projects were billed as the country's answer to solve future shortages. But they would be beset with delays, cost overruns and rampant corruption.

'It's what happens when politicians interfere,' Oberholzer said. 'If you look at it today, it's incredible. So that's what I can remember at the time, we were told [by government prior to starting the projects], please note, stay in your lane, we will as government decide on the power stations and who will build it. Up until the pawpaw hit the fan, and then it was, Eskom, get going. A lot of people are crucifying Eskom, I believe unnecessarily. If you take Kusile, it's the fourth biggest power station in the world. How do you build a power station while you are designing it? You need five years at least to plan this blinking thing, but we had no luxury like that. Everybody is crucifying Eskom, and no one in government is standing up and saying, please, point some fingers back to us. We put Eskom in the position that they are in today.'

When Kusile and Medupi broke ground, Eskom had not built power stations for decades. In the 1970s and 1980s, the utility had a team of roughly 3 000 people dedicated to building power stations one after the other.

'It was a well-oiled machine,' Oberholzer recalled. 'Now in 20 years, lots of those people had passed on or moved on. We had to build these power stations with virtually no experience and zero skills.'

So Eskom appointed engineering panels, A, B and C, to help them.

'But this is what people don't understand, we had to make plans. Because the country was in dire need of power, but it doesn't take away that we botched it up. And what no one is saying, we were running out of money, so some of the progress, some of these projects, were put on hold. Nobody will talk about it. And this is what irritates me about these energy experts and all these other people who have a lot to say, they selectively make up [i.e. they are selective about what they say], but they don't give truth,' Oberholzer said. 'And remember, the focus was not on really giving all the attention to finishing these projects, it was also to line pockets.'

The Eskom Files have revealed the deep-seated rot at Kusile – how Eskom officials colluded with contractors to inflate claims and how, in return, they were paid more than R100 million through a slush fund. It is likely that similar events took place at Medupi and Ingula, which are yet to be fully probed.

Oberholzer was the person who took the business case for these projects to the board in 2006 and 2007. Ingula was meant to cost R13.4 billion. It's closer to R30 billion today. Medupi was meant to cost R68 billion. It will cost double that to finish. Kusile, similarly, will cost an estimated R160 billion to complete.

There have been countless controversies around these power stations, but none as insidious as the role of the ANC and its investment arm, Chancellor House, which held a stake in a local company established by Japanese heavy industries conglomerate Hitachi.[2] Chancellor House was awarded a 25 per cent shareholding in Hitachi Power Africa in November

2005 in exchange for $192 000, according to a US Securities and Exchange Commission (SEC) complaint filed in a Washington court in 2015.[3] Less than two years later, Hitachi won the tender to build six boilers for Medupi, which would later be extended to Kusile under a so-called 'fleet strategy'. The contract was worth roughly R40 billion.

Nine years later, in 2014, as scrutiny mounted, Chancellor House relinquished its stake in Hitachi Power Africa. It had earned in the region of $10 million in this time for success fees, dividends and for the share buyout. It had secured a roughly 5 000 per cent return on its original investment, for contributing nothing but its political connections to the deal with Eskom. Chancellor House did not employ a single engineer, welder or project manager. It was merely along for the ride, to fulfil black economic empowerment requirements.[4]

In 2015, Hitachi paid $19 million to the SEC to settle its claim, with an important caveat – Hitachi could never again deny any wrongdoing with the Chancellor House deal, or it would face a fresh prosecution of the SEC complaint.

The deal has never been properly investigated by any South African authorities.

News of the deal between Chancellor House and Hitachi, and the former's numerous links to the ANC, was first broken in 2007 by investigative reporters Sam Sole and Stefaans Brümmer of the *Mail & Guardian*. Despite their shining a light on the issue, the deal went ahead. Valli Moosa was chairperson of Eskom at the time, while also serving on the ANC's national executive committee. The party has maintained denials that it was in any way involved and said that questions should be directed to Chancellor House.

Fourteen years later, the boilers are yet to be finished at Kusile, while extensive fixes have had to be made to boilers already built to rectify design defects. The boilers, which stand at 130 metres tall, are effectively too short and get too hot near the top, creating exhaust steam temperatures that are excessive – roughly 128 degrees Celsius.

'That's too hot and it's damaging the exhaust equipment. That's why we can't operate the units to their full capacity,' De Ruyter told Parliament in 2020.[5] It will require each of the 12 boilers to be modified and built 12.5 metres taller, modifications that will be implemented prior to the completion of the last three Kusile units and retroactively done on completed boilers at Medupi and Kusile. Each fix will require a 75-day shutdown, during which modifications to coal mills and other sections of the plant will also be undertaken.

It is a problem, Oberholzer said, born of the truncated design period – just a year, where normally it would have taken three years. There was another problem – to successfully execute the major new build projects, Eskom had to outsource nearly all the planning and design work in addition to appointing the contractors that would undertake the actual building and engineering work.

It was around the time that the ANC's role was first uncovered that Oberholzer, a key part of the Eskom team responsible for managing the build projects, was in Dublin, in June 2008. He was visiting ESBI, one of Eskom's panel of engineers, established because the technical expertise needed to build power stations simply did not exist within Eskom any more. The purpose of the working visit was to look at wind farms in Ireland and talk to ESBI about the Sere wind farm, Eskom's very first renewable energy project, in the Western Cape.

'I was sick and tired of a lot of things at Eskom,' Oberholzer recalled. 'I was not in sync, while I was heading up group capital, with the decisions. One of those decisions was to appoint Hitachi, and I needed to sign the contract. And I said no. I didn't want to be associated with something that the ruling party of the day had a significant share in ... and that I needed to sign that. And I needed to take it to the board for approval.'

The Hitachi contract was the straw that broke the camel's back.

'For me it just didn't make sense, that certain contracts were pushed, and that we had to look, I wouldn't say with different eyes, but it was clear there was government interference in some of these major contracts. Do

I have tangible proof? No. But man, you don't … it's very clear to see things,' he said.

Initially, the boiler contract had been awarded to Alstom, a French company, which had also won the contracts for the turbines. But the decision was made, ostensibly after Alstom raised the possibility of constraints, to re-award the boiler contract to Hitachi. Hitachi was initially asked to build the boilers for Medupi, but this was later expanded, without any tender process.

There were other problems, too.

'I can remember the first breakaway we had as a team, it would have been late 2007 or early 2008, but it was the management team of Eskom Enterprises, of which I was one, [we] went to the Riviera hotel next to the Vaal. And when we introduced ourselves, everybody had to say something, and Brian stood up and said, I am Brian Dames, and I trust no one,' Oberholzer recalled. 'This is now your leader, saying I don't trust you. Then I realised. I had difficulty stomaching his arrogance, I had big issues with him trying to centralise everything, because of his makeup, you know, I don't trust anybody, and that created the vehicle in this organisation to steal.'

Sitting in his hotel room in Dublin one night, Oberholzer wrote to Dames, his boss at the time who would later become Eskom CEO, and told him he was resigning and would be leaving at the end of 2008. He copied in the then chief executive, Jacob Maroga.

'I came back from the business visit, and nothing happened. And I said, okay, that's fine. On 17 November 2008, I tabled my resignation, then all of a sudden everything happened, you know, why, what is wrong with you, et cetera. And I said to him, but I wrote you a letter, I gave you six months' notice I am going to leave, so that you can get someone in my place. You just again ignored me,' Oberholzer recalled.

Dames, he said, was adamant that he could not leave. He got the board together and offered Oberholzer a promotion from general manager to senior general manager. His family was already at the coast waiting for him and Dames offered to pay for him to go down for a weekend in early December. Oberholzer, however, would not be swayed and returned that Monday with his final answer: he would be leaving.

'I left this organisation after 26 years, without a thank you and a cup of coffee. This shows you the Brian Dames I experienced; this is why I have no respect for him. And he said to me after I left, you can always come back, and I just thought, *ag*, fuck you, man. Needless to say, I was hurt. I was very upset with God. Because my dad 25 years, and me 26, and we didn't overlap, so we gave more than 50 years for the company, for the country, so I said, why?'

By his own admission, his experience with Dames and the reasons for his departure made Oberholzer bitter with Eskom, and he ended up cutting ties, even refraining from following the news around Eskom for some years.

'I did pick up now and then some bits of arrogant Koko and the idiotic statements Brian Molefe made, you know, just look how great I am and we stopped load shedding and all this bullshit. That's the only thing I sort of followed,' he recalled.

Oberholzer would spend a decade outside Eskom, initially working for Stefanutti Stocks where, after four years, he realised he was not cut out to be a contractor. He left and started his own business, landing some work in Zambia where, he said, he 'really learned what corruption is about and what these international companies would do to secure work'.

In early 2018, he got a call from an Eskom board member asking him to come back to the utility to help turn the ship around. He was reluctant at first, but he set about studying the financials and soon realised that things were not going well. After five weeks of deep thought, he relented.

'Lindy had planted the seed in my mind,' he said, 'you know, that this call had come from God. And eventually I thought to myself, well, if my purpose in life is as I had realised so many years before, to contribute positively, this was perhaps my chance to plough back into Eskom my years of experience and knowledge.'

He was interviewed by the board and undertook a psychometric examination.

'I had decided one day to visit my cousin in the Boksburg, Benoni area and just as I pulled up to the house my phone rang, and it was a number I did not recognise. But it was Phakamani [Hadebe, the then chief executive of Eskom], who asked me, you know, when can you start?'

On 16 July 2018, after a 10-year hiatus, Oberholzer returned to Eskom, now as the second-most senior executive in the company. It was on that first day, he said, that he realised just how bad things were – there was load shedding at the time and a massive strike by union members.

'It was an incredible culture shock when I arrived back at Eskom, because what the board said to me the challenges were, they didn't even know a tenth of what the issues really were.'

Oberholzer had returned to an Eskom reeling from the aftershocks of state capture. On his first day back, he called for individual meetings with the executives who would be reporting to him. In a series of one-hour sessions with each of them, he began to understand just how deep the challenges were.

'If I had still been drinking at that point, I probably would have gone off on my own with a bottle. I admit I thought what the hell was I thinking coming back.'

Oberholzer set about getting reports from each of the divisions to assess the current state of play. After reading the reports, he identified several immediate problems, and picked up that, on the transmission side of the business, there was a looming crisis that could potentially lead to a disaster on the scale of load shedding.

'We have infrastructure there sometimes more than 48 years old. And there simply wasn't any maintenance. If you look at the performance figures, transmission was going south quickly. But fortunately, in the last two years or so, we have managed to turn that around,' Oberholzer told me.

The incidents and issues that required attention quickly multiplied, and every day people would approach him with information about issues that needed to be investigated. Early on, he visited power stations and examined some of the issues people had raised with him, and soon started uncovering major problems – caused by corruption, neglect or incompetence, or a combination thereof.

He decided to visit a warehouse where certain high-value, strategic spares and parts were kept – its location is closely guarded, but, according to Oberholzer, the facility, built by the apartheid government, is like a massive bomb shelter with metre-thick concrete walls and massive steel doors. It is located near one of the power stations and he was aware, peripherally, that the store contained spares worth more than R20 billion. Some officials, he said, were reluctant to organise the visit. So at 7 a.m. one Monday morning, he set off and arrived at the facility unannounced.

'As I drove up, I could see one of the massive steel doors sort of hanging, broken, to one side. A guy came ambling up to me, chewing a piece of gum, and I told him who I was and what I was doing there. I proceeded inside.'

He found a clear layer of dust on everything. Wooden crates of spares had been broken open, the expensive, sometimes nearly irreplaceable strategic parts stripped of the copper inside them. Towards the rear of the facility, weeds and grass had started growing through the concrete to knee height. Parts lay scattered among the growth.

'I asked the guy who was sitting there, do you have a computer where I can check the inventory? No computer. Do you have a book, something? He didn't. Some of those parts were supposed to be preserved.'

As Oberholzer came walking back out of the facility, having seen the state of it, the power station manager arrived.

'I think they must have seen the look on my face. Because they immediately just threw up their hands and said they weren't accountable for the facility.'

It was only after Oberholzer asked the procurement boss at head office to find out who was responsible for the warehouse that the same manager realised it was his responsibility.

Oberholzer uncovered a plethora of disgraceful lapses – including the basics, such as Eskom paying R54 for a single black bag, R22 for a roll of single-ply toilet paper and double that for a litre of milk.

'I visited the distribution centre in King William's Town, and the one guy there said to me, you people at head office don't know what you are doing. He explained that if he wanted to buy coffee or milk, he had to get it delivered from Johannesburg, where he could buy it locally for half the price. And that's when I realised there were middlemen everywhere making a fortune,' Oberholzer said. In those early days, he made it a priority to start relinking procurement of such basic goods to power stations and offices, decentralising it all.

But contracts for milk and sugar, while emblematic of Eskom's state, were not the biggest problems he would have to deal with.

'I nearly fell on my back when I found out that the costs for Medupi and Kusile had basically doubled. It just couldn't be, I thought to myself.'

Twenty-three days after he returned to Eskom, Oberholzer signed a mandate for Bowmans law firm to investigate several key contracts at Kusile, including the turbine contract originally awarded to Alstom, which was bought by General Electric; the boiler contract awarded to Hitachi, since ceded to Mitsubishi; as well as civil construction contracts awarded to Tubular and his former employer, Stefanutti Stocks. He had learned that there were major problems with these contracts from people who had approached him with information during his first days in office.

He had set in motion the first steps of a major war with deeply entrenched networks.

'I remember visiting Kusile one day, and in the mess hall I engaged with staff, and I told them, corruption was a major problem,' Oberholzer recalled. 'And one or two arrogant people challenged me, and said, you know, so what are you saying? My response was simple. Just watch the scoreboard, and you will understand.'

It would take just four months for the first attack on Oberholzer to begin, when Jabulane Mavimbela, the power station manager of Tutuka, filed a grievance against him, as well as acting head of generation Andrew Etzinger and a senior official brought in to help steer generation in the right direction, Chris Schutte. Mavimbela accused them of victimisation and harassment, motivated, he said, by racism.

Prior to this, all three men had spoken with Mavimbela about the performance of Tutuka, which was floundering. The power station had become Eskom's worst-performing station, with regular breakdowns. The utility had also uncovered rampant corruption that apparently flourished under Mavimbela's watch, including the theft of hundreds of millions of rands' worth of fuel oil and spares. Arrests had been made concerning an alleged syndicate involved in pilfering the spares, while Eskom said more arrests would follow regarding the fuel oil.

In his report to then CEO Hadebe on 5 March 2019, Advocate Khotso Ramolefe dismissed the grievances because the issues that had caused Mavimbela to feel aggrieved had dissipated.

'Observing and listening to Mr Mavimbela, I gained the distinct impression that he rather appears to lack sufficient skills not only to resolve conflict, but he does not seem to have used to his benefit at least, one immediate avenue for conflict resolution such as asking for a meeting with the other employees in order to ascertain such problems as they had with him, any concerns that he had in relation to them, and to find ways to resolve all these in a manner that asserts him as a manager,' Ramolefe wrote.[6]

'Regrettably, his failure to do this noticeably weakened his position as the complainant and could well continue to do so in future if the lack of this particular skill persists. Mr Mavimbela also found it easy to play the race card by referring, during his representations, to his "black skin" as an explanation for the treatment by the other employees who all happen to be white.

'At this point, I must say it was rather unfortunate to see Mr Mavimbela at a complete loss for words as soon as all three employees, not once but a few times each spontaneously offered him their apologies for the perception he had that they had meant to be disrespectful towards him. Two things were made absolutely clear to him though: one, none of the three employees were prepared to apologise for having spoken with him about the need for Tutuka to run efficiently.'

Ramolefe singled out Oberholzer in this regard, who, he wrote, 'made clear his passion to see Eskom get out of its current problems. This passion shone in significance when compared with Mr Mavimbela's concern on the other hand, which was ultimately about issues more personal than professional.'

Ramolefe also noted that Mavimbela 'was told quite categorically to avoid playing the race card, all three employees having disavowed themselves of racism'.

The grievance was resolved, in Ramolefe's view, because Mavimbela's chief complaint that he had been replaced while on leave by Dennis Child was unfounded. Child had been brought in by Etzinger during December 2018 because Mavimbela had been on leave and departed Tutuka immediately on his return. He recommended that levels of support for generation officials be increased, and Oberholzer concurred with a request from Mavimbela that Etzinger be replaced by someone more experienced in generation, namely Bheki Nxumalo or Phillip Dukashe.

'Etzinger was just carrying the baton,' Oberholzer explained to me. 'And I have huge respect for him saying, even though he was not experienced in generation, to put up his hand and say I will give it a shot.'

But Oberholzer's biggest fights were yet to come. Over the next three years, he would face investigations by forensic firm Crawford Independent Associate over contracts he had signed in 2008, specifically for engineering consultants Black & Veatch, who ultimately oversaw the design and construction of Kusile Power Station, in a remarkably flawed probe that seemingly ignored several modifications to the contract that occurred during Oberholzer's time in the private sector.

He would be investigated for a raft of allegations, including nepotism, for allegedly pressuring an Eskom official into making a R40-million payment to construction company Aveng, hired to undertake the Majuba rail project, and for allegedly failing to declare a shareholding in Stefanutti Stocks to Eskom and then meeting with his former employer. He would also be investigated for an instruction for Eskom to pay General Electric, a subcontractor to Group Five on the Ankerlig Transmission Koeberg Second Supply Project, for turbines they were supplying. ATKSS will see several small gas-powered turbines built to ensure a back-up energy supply that can be quickly brought online to help Koeberg during start-ups. This project has taken nearly a decade to finalise, in circumstances where a similar project was undertaken in California with the same General Electric turbines in just 42 days, as Gordhan pointed out.[7]

Advocate Nazeer Cassim would be appointed by Eskom to probe the allegations, which, apart from the Stefanutti Stocks issue, chiefly stemmed from one grievance filed against Oberholzer by the now late Mark Chettiar, the former manager of coal and clean technologies who had oversight of the project and who would later be described as the 'leading protagonist' in the attacks on Oberholzer. Chettiar's allegations would be investigated by not only Cassim but also De Ruyter, the Zondo Commission, the SIU and the Public Protector, all of whom would clear Oberholzer of any wrongdoing.

4

The report

IN AUGUST 2019, TWO REPRESENTATIVES of the Zondo Commission – the head of investigations, Terence Nombembe, and the Eskom investigation lead, Jabu Mahlangu – held a meeting with Eskom head of legal Bartlett Hewu and acting CEO and board chairperson Jabu Mabuza.

The purpose of the meeting was simple – the Zondo Commission had been tipped off about 'certain pending transactions' and, after an initial investigation, had decided to issue a report detailing some preliminary findings and recommendations. They were there to hand over the document.[1]

The 33-page report was handed to Hewu, setting in motion a chain of events that would culminate in Eskom paying R26 million in legal costs and claims – costs that could have been avoided had anyone realised the allegations were false and designed not to ensure accountability, but to malign senior officials working to clean up corruption. The report sparked calls for Oberholzer's resignation and set a dark cloud over one of Eskom's top senior contracts management specialists, Dr Danie Möller, who has worked tirelessly to save Eskom billions in claims from contractors.[2]

It all began far away from the glare of the media spotlight when senior Eskom official Mark Chettiar quietly approached the Zondo Commission in May and June 2019 with allegations against Oberholzer and Möller that centred on a R40-million potential payment to construction company Aveng, linked to the Majuba rail project.[3] Chettiar had more than 20 years of service at the power utility when, in May 2018, he was made acting general manager for coal and clean technologies projects, a section under Eskom's group capital division responsible for major projects in generation. He was appointed by the group executive for group capital,

Abram Masango, who resigned from Eskom in October 2018 and who would later be arrested as part of the corruption probe relating to alleged kickbacks paid by Kusile supplier Tubular.

In his new position, Chettiar had ultimate oversight of several major projects at Eskom's power stations, most of which have made headlines in recent years due to their impact on the utility's overall performance and their contribution to load shedding. One of the key projects under Chettiar's portfolio was the Majuba railway line.

After Masango's departure, Eskom's leadership, which by then included Hadebe, decided not to fill the position, and Oberholzer was instead asked to oversee the division in addition to his duties as COO.

According to an August 2020 report by De Ruyter, the result of a third investigation into the allegations against Oberholzer, the decision to ask Oberholzer to manage the group capital division was to enable him to understand and deal with corruption within the division, as well as to manage underperformance of key projects and a scaling down of new build activities. In short, Oberholzer was asked to shake group capital until all the bad apples had fallen out and the projects that were costing Eskom millions it did not have started to see some form of tangible progress. By all accounts, he did just that. This decision also made him Chettiar's direct manager.

Chettiar had inherited projects with major problems, the Majuba railway being one of them. The clash between him and Oberholzer arose when, after almost a year, there was still no turnaround. Things percolated until early September 2019, when, during a phone call, Oberholzer allegedly asked Chettiar to consider whether he 'was cut out for the job'. This prompted Chettiar to file a grievance in mid-September in which he made a range of serious allegations against Oberholzer. Chettiar accused him of victimisation, alleging that Oberholzer had started mistreating him after his disclosures to the Zondo Commission investigators and their subsequent report to Eskom. It was apparent from the report that Chettiar had taken particular umbrage with the actions of Dr Danie

Möller in the contracts management office, allegations he repeated in his grievance.

Here it is necessary to take a step back and delve into the history of the Majuba rail project to understand not only Oberholzer's frustrations with Chettiar, but also why tenuous allegations against him were accepted with little regard for the facts. Industry expert, journalist and managing editor of EE Publishers Chris Yelland has called the project 'a debacle' that foreshadowed the difficulties Eskom would face in managing major projects in subsequent years.[4]

Majuba Power Station is situated near the small town of Amersfoort in Mpumalanga and is the last of Eskom's major historical builds to come online – the first of six units of the 4 100 MW station was commissioned in 1996, the final in 2001.

Traditionally, Eskom built many of its power stations near coal deposits that could be mined and moved to the station by overland conveyors, by far the cheapest way to transport coal. Some stations were specifically designed to accommodate the quality of the coal from these mines, which were known as tied collieries. The Majuba Colliery, which was to have been operated by Rand Mining, was destined for disaster.

In 1993, while underground works to establish the mine were under way, geological faults were discovered that would make mining large quantities of coal difficult and dangerous. 'All Eskom had to do was speak to people in the area,' one official recently told me. 'Even the farmers knew about the faults and could have advised Eskom not to try and mine there.'[5]

But construction of the power station had already started. The discovery of the fault meant Majuba would suffer from challenges around coal supply for the duration of its life.

'As a result of the decommissioning of Majuba Colliery, a branch rail link with a capacity of 8 metric tons per annum was built from Palmford on the Natal Corridor (Natcor) general freight line between Standerton and Volksrust, to Majuba power station,' Yelland wrote in August 2020. 'Due to a surplus of Eskom generation capacity at that time, the construction of Majuba was deliberately delayed, and at the end of the second quarter of 1996, only the first unit was in commercial operation. The capacity of the Palmford rail link from the Natcor line was therefore more than adequate to meet the initial coal supply requirements of Majuba power station.'

Then, in the early 2000s, Eskom established a policy of procuring coal from diverse, emerging sources, not just the traditional large mining houses. While the Palmford line could still provide Majuba with the coal it needed, the location of these new miners meant transporting the coal by rail would be impossible. Delivery by road then displaced rail deliveries, Yelland noted.

In 2004, Eskom put in motion plans to build a new railway line to transport coal to Majuba. In December that year, the plans were approved for the R1.5-billion, 68-kilometre rail line that would link near Ermelo to the major coal freight line running from Mpumalanga to the Richards Bay Coal Terminal and thereby ensure a more reliable and cheaper means of coal transport from the emerging suppliers. The project, however, experienced several challenges.

'These include delays in land acquisition for the rail servitude, funding constraints (which finally resulted in R6-billion allocation in a $3.75-billion loan to Eskom by the World Bank in 2010), unforeseen underground conditions, adverse weather conditions, scope changes, and disruptions by community pressure groups,' Yelland wrote, noting that the contract for the upgrading of the coal stockyard and the interface with the power station had to be issued to the market three times, due to a lack of responses.

As a result, by 2017, after more than a decade, the project was still unfinished and the upgrade of the coal stockyard at Majuba to accommodate the new line was still outstanding. It was in early 2017 that Aveng was awarded a R517-million (R590 million with contingency) contract to upgrade the coal stockyard, which included the design and installation of a new coal tippler – a large machine that picks up and empties rail cars filled with coal. Majuba is the only power station that uses a tippler.

The Aveng contract was originally meant to conclude in early 2018,

222 days after it began, but quickly ran into its own challenges – some caused by Eskom, which on numerous occasions had to postpone a critical shutdown for 40 days because it had been unable to stockpile enough coal to supply Majuba while the shutdown was ongoing.

In May 2018, when Chettiar was appointed, Eskom had already postponed the shutdown once, moving the start date from March to September 2018. During his tenure it would be moved again, to 19 December 2018. The postponements were accommodated by shifting the contract's completion date.

In December 2018, Eskom tried to move the date of the shutdown once again, to early January 2019. When Aveng responded that it could not mobilise resources at such short notice, and during the annual builders' break, Eskom blamed Aveng for the delays. But Aveng had had enough.

In a lengthy, nine-page letter to Oberholzer on 22 January 2019, Grant Stock, group commercial executive for Aveng, pointed out that they had repeatedly asked Eskom to give the company at least three months' notice before the planned shutdown commenced, mainly due to the need for Aveng to ensure its subcontractors were available and to remobilise its resources to the site. In the letter, Stock also aired numerous other issues around the way the contract had been managed. Over the course of 2018, Aveng had notified Eskom of potential claims stemming from the time extensions, and in the letter to Oberholzer, Stock set out their dissatisfaction with how the notifications and correspondence had been dealt with.

'The contractor [Aveng] addresses its concerns with regard to the egregious manner in which the project manager and Eskom has conducted itself in the administration of the contract,' Stock wrote. 'The conduct of the project manager and Eskom in our view evidence a general disregard of the fundamental obligation under the contract for the parties to act in a spirit of mutual trust and cooperation.'

Stock said the issues went beyond a 'simple breach of the contract'. Aveng felt that 'Eskom is not, and does not intend, abiding by the terms of the contract'.

'The end result is that terms of the contract have become irrelevant, supplanted by the whims and needs of Eskom alone with little or no consideration to the consequences to the contractor and its subcontractors,' Stock continued.

He also outlined Aveng's concerns over non-payment of compensation events, an apparent failure by the project manager to respond to official correspondence, and non-payment of the retention monies in circumstances where a retention bond had been provided to Eskom.

Compensation events are events that are usually not the fault of the contractor and change the cost of the work, or the time needed to complete it. In such cases, the contractor is entitled to be compensated for any effect the event has on the price or completion date. To provide protection for the employer, contracts also include provisions for money to be held back from each payment, known as retention, in case the contractor does not complete the work or does not complete it to the satisfaction of all parties. But Aveng had exercised an option in the contract to provide Eskom with a retention bond – essentially an insurance policy to cover the value of the retention – to free up the retention monies held by the utility. Nearly a year later, Eskom had yet to release just over R21 million in retention funds to Aveng.

'Contrary to the spirit of the contract, the employer [Eskom] and the project manager's actions regarding the commencement of the shutdown works and the failure to certify compensation events has forced the contractor to commence dispute proceedings to obtain payment,' Stock wrote.

To this end, Aveng had filed a statement of claims to an independent adjudicator, Ian Massey, amounting to R130 million: R81 million stemming from the extension of the contract completion date; two claims of just over R3 million each for subcontractor costs; the R21-million claim for retention money; and a R22-million claim for changes to the tippler design.

Requesting an urgent meeting with Oberholzer to resolve the problems, Stock warned that if Eskom was not able to address the issues satisfactorily, Aveng would contemplate giving the utility notice of its repudiation of the contract.

Oberholzer, recognising the urgency of the matter, quickly convened a meeting on 14 February 2019, while also responding to the letter, denying Eskom's responsibility for the claims.

The minutes of the meeting show that Oberholzer apologised to Aveng for the poor manner in which the contract had been managed. He mandated Chettiar to urgently resolve the non-payment of retention monies, and further delegated Danie Möller to engage with Aveng with a view to resolve the issues around the compensation claims.

Aveng had a strong position. Eskom's project manager on the Majuba rail project *had* failed to respond appropriately and within the contractual time frames to the notifications filed during 2018, leading Aveng to argue that some of the claims were deemed accepted due to the late responses and placing Eskom in a precarious position when the claims were eventually brought before an adjudicator in early 2019.

After the time frames for deemed acceptance lapsed, Aveng was contractually entitled to include the amounts it had quoted for compensation events in its interim payment certificates (IPCs). IPCs are, as the name suggests, interim. The payments are made and the argument is had afterwards. These types of construction contracts are managed this way to prevent work stoppages resulting from disputes over payment or cash-flow issues. Legally, both parties can challenge the amounts at a later stage, and processes for how this must be done are clearly defined in the contract. But the project manager refused to certify the IPCs, leading to at least one claim that Eskom could not rationally defend.

Regarding the retention monies, in the case of the Aveng/Eskom deal, 50 per cent of the contract was to be retention-free, and Aveng could elect to either allow Eskom to keep back 10 per cent of each payment until the contract was finished or provide a retention bond. In this case, the value of the bond would be 10 per cent of 50 per cent of the contract value (because 50 per cent was to be retention-free).

Providing a bond is legally binding on the contractor. The employer, in this case Eskom, can theoretically claim any value under the bond if the work is not completed. Aveng initially opted to allow Eskom to keep back 10 per cent of each payment, which by late 2018 amounted to R27 million. But, due to the numerous extensions and delays, Aveng was facing a cash-flow issue on the project and elected to provide a bond so that the R27 million could be released to ease the financial strain. For reasons that remain unclear to this day, for months after the bond was issued, Eskom simply did not release the money.

It took Oberholzer's intervention for Chettiar to release the funds, only for Chettiar to later claim he did so under duress and pressure in circumstances where 'risk and governance' had advised that Eskom should not release the retention money – a bizarre statement in its own right, as, contractually, Eskom had no choice. The money was owed to Aveng for work already done, and in any case, Eskom had a legally enforceable bond for close to R90 million.

A few days after the February meeting, Aveng chief executive Sean Flanagan emailed Oberholzer to 'thank [him] for the first genuinely positive engagement we have had with Eskom for a long time'. Flanagan said he had arrived at the meeting intent on appealing to Oberholzer to 'accept the reality of the crisis of this project' and the 'impact of Eskom's conduct on the project and our business and that of our subcontractors ... Against my initial scepticism, we left the meeting feeling that you had heard us, that you personally want this properly dealt with and resolved and, for the first time on this project, our team has started to feel optimistic that we can get somewhere by talking.'

He concluded: 'Although Aveng must reserve its rights and the contract and dispute resolution processes continue, I am confident that we have broken through a barrier today.'

Aveng's early optimism, however, was misplaced.

Chettiar was incensed by Oberholzer's apology to Aveng during the meeting. He felt undermined and under pressure to pay the retention funds. He addressed this with Oberholzer after the meeting, and documents show that he authored a memorandum motivating the release of the retention money on 22 February, a little over a week after first being instructed by Oberholzer to do so.

Möller and his team, meanwhile, sprang into action immediately after the February meeting. The deadline to file an official response to Aveng's claims was 27 February, and time was already against them. If Eskom failed to file a response in time, adjudicator Ian Massey could simply award the claims to Aveng, and Eskom would then have to file a notice of dissatisfaction to take the matter to arbitration or approach the courts. Both options would incur considerable legal costs.

Led by Möller, the team managed to reduce Aveng's claims from R129 million to just over R60 million. While the two smallest claims, for subcontractor costs, remained largely unchanged, the claim around the design change to the tippler was scrapped. The claim had originated from Aveng subcontractor Tenova Mining & Minerals, which had designed and manufactured the indexer for the tippler. It was the design of the indexer that apparently had to be changed. Aveng was unable to provide substantiation for the claim and it was agreed it would be dealt with in a separate process.

Möller and his team were able to reduce the largest claim ('Claim 2') – for the time extension – to just over R40 million. Assisted by a professional claims analyst, they had determined that, in their view, Aveng was entitled to just under half of the R81 million claimed. On 9 May 2019, Flanagan wrote in an email to Oberholzer that Aveng would 'accept a settlement of R43 million for this portion of the claim if payment is made by end May 2019'. This included R40 million for the time extension and R3 million for the two smaller claims.

On 13 May, Flanagan wrote again, stating that good progress had been made in the discussions to resolve the claims, but, he said, 'the pressing issue is that even though Aveng is prepared to agree to Eskom's revised settlement value of R40 million ... the proposed Eskom approval timeline makes it impossible to do so! The Eskom approval process extends into July on worst case scenario ... Aveng cannot suspend the adjudication proceedings for several months with the risk that the settlement proposal will not be approved by Eskom.'

Oberholzer responded on 18 May and said that, while he understood Aveng's need to meet its financial obligations, 'Eskom as a state-owned company must follow corporate governance processes ... the approval of the settlement offer of R40 million requires us to obtain approval for both internal and external governance processes.' Oberholzer also proposed a timeline, saying Eskom was doing 'our best to expedite the approvals as much as we can without contravening the governance processes'.

Flanagan was not convinced. On 22 May, he replied, saying Aveng had no choice but to proceed with the adjudication process. Eskom never responded and instead, on 23 May, filed its written submissions relating to Claim 2, which included the assessment of R40 million. Aveng accepted Eskom's assessment and requested that Massey formally make the award for this amount – which he subsequently did on 30 May. Eskom did not file a notice of dissatisfaction with Massey's award, arguably because it stood to pay substantially more if arbitration proceedings went Aveng's way, and it was clear that Eskom had been responsible for the lion's share of the delays. Now they had to pay.

It was the prospective payment of this R40 million that Chettiar would later allege was unlawful, as, according to him, Möller and his team had acted without a mandate in entering into a settlement agreement with Aveng. But documents, including a High Court judgment and a second adjudicator's award, show that Chettiar was wrong. There had never been a settlement. In any case, Chettiar and his team were ultimately responsible for managing the dispute process and could have filed a notice of dissatisfaction. Instead, Chettiar argued belatedly and in other forums, including in his submissions to the Zondo Commission, that Möller and his team had 'interfered' in the process – despite claims settlements of this nature being a major part of the mandate of the contracts management office and an area in which Möller had substantial experience.

Despite Chettiar's contentions that the claims settlement was irregular, documents show Möller always acted within his scope and mandate, and furthermore achieved substantial savings for Eskom. Conservative estimates show that Möller and his team have, in the past three years alone, saved Eskom more than R2 billion in claims from major construction companies. The actual figure may be far higher, but due to confidentiality around these processes, documentary proof is difficult to obtain. By all accounts, he is involved in defending massive claims against several major Eskom suppliers on Medupi and Kusile.

Resolving the claims process with Aveng was just one part of the risk Eskom had to mitigate. If Aveng walked away from the contract, as it had threatened to do in January, it would take Eskom more than a year to appoint a new contractor through tender processes and allow time for the work to be completed. In the meantime, Eskom was paying approximately R270 000 a day for trucks to transport coal to Majuba Power Station, coal that had serious quality risks and was causing increased breakdowns within the power plant.

In all his complaints and submissions, it seems Chettiar never once mentioned these factors. His primary focus was on preventing the payment to Aveng. Möller, on the other hand, apparently recognising the risks, started negotiations with a view to settle the disputes amicably, outside of the adjudication process, to keep the project on track.

And he had considerable success.

A key document that Chettiar relied on to bolster his views was a March 2019 audit and forensics report that was never made public or used in any proceedings, as it was only ever meant for internal use. The report inexplicably determined that Aveng's claims were invalid, based on outdated information around the outages on site. The document, in short, was not worth the paper it was printed on – it was signed and submitted in March 2019, and the latest, incomplete information in the report was from prior to October 2018.

It was shortly after the adjudicator's award confirming that Eskom had to pay the R40 million that, in June, Chettiar made a written submission to the Zondo Commission, specifically highlighting the Aveng payment, and claiming that Möller had acted without an approved mandate and that the amount had been reached by Möller and his team 'to the exclusion' of the project management team. Yet documents in the Eskom Files show more than 70 emails between Möller, his team and the project management team, as well as Chettiar, who was copied in on most of the correspondence, some of which refers to meetings and phone calls between the two teams.

By mid-July 2019, the amount had still not been paid to Aveng. In a letter dated 19 July, Aveng accused Eskom of repudiation of contract. Two days later, the then project manager, Themba Khumalo, drafted a memorandum seeking permission to obtain external legal advice on whether or not Eskom should pay based on the adjudicator's award. The memorandum detailed that internal Eskom governance procedures had already been started to seek approval for the payment to be made. A week later, law firm ENSafrica provided their legal opinion: Eskom had to pay due to their earlier non-conformance to processes.[6]

On 13 August, Aveng launched a High Court application seeking an order forcing Eskom to pay. Oberholzer wrote to Aveng, saying that Eskom was hoping to conclude its internal processes to make payment in the first week of September, and asking for the court process to be suspended. Aveng refused.

Then, on 21 August, Chettiar's disclosures to the Zondo Commission bore fruit. The commission's investigators, at a meeting with Mabuza and head of legal Bartlett Hewu, handed over their report, recommending that Eskom should not pay Aveng until the allegations, made by Chettiar, were fully investigated.

Despite his contentions that he had never supported the payment of the R40 million, it was around this time that Chettiar endorsed a memorandum seeking approval for the payment. But now Oberholzer declined to support the payment. In a handwritten note next to his signature, Oberholzer stated that a report by the Zondo Commission had recommended that Eskom should not pay. Tellingly, Oberholzer himself only set eyes on the report in July 2020. Up until then, he had merely been informed of its recommendations.

A copy of the report, which was subsequently leaked to News24 as part of the Eskom Files, raised more questions than answers. It made no findings or recommendations concerning Oberholzer, effectively clearing him of wrongdoing. But the final 10 pages of the report, which according to the index dealt with another major tender for the battery energy storage system, were – and remain – missing.

There were other problems. It transpired that the report wasn't a report of the commission at all, and that deputy chief justice Raymond Zondo, the head of the commission, had never signed off on it. Zondo was later appointed chief justice in March 2022. Furthermore, nearly every allegation the investigators relied on in reaching their conclusions was false or missing proper context, which they apparently failed to clarify or understand fully. It was also troubling that the commission had taken the step of submitting a report to Eskom when it had not done anything similar during the entire period of its existence.

Years later, the commission's secretary, Professor Itumeleng Mosala, would be at pains to clarify that the document was not a report of the commission but rather a 'discussion document', despite the authors referring to it as an 'interim report'.

The report itself was apparently not widely distributed, presumably because it made no findings against Oberholzer, despite the entire premise of Chettiar's disclosures to the Zondo Commission being designed to implicate the COO in wrongdoing. Möller, however, a key official working to counter efforts of extraction disguised as claims, was thrown under the bus – the commission recommended further investigation into his role and agreed with Chettiar that he had acted without a mandate. The allegations that Möller was corrupt circulated widely within Eskom. He was subsequently cleared by an internal probe, after his prophetic warnings over additional costs to the utility proved accurate.

In early September 2019, Oberholzer received 'another surprise' on one of the projects Chettiar was managing – the building of a new ash dam at Camden Power Station. A significant oversight in the project's planning had led to additional work being identified, resulting in costs nearly doubling. Oberholzer, infuriated, called Chettiar the following morning. It was during this phone conversation that Oberholzer asked Chettiar to consider whether he was cut out for his job.

A few weeks later, in mid-September, Chettiar filed his grievance, repeating many of the allegations he had made to the Zondo Commission's investigators.

5

The investigation

JABU MABUZA, THE ESKOM CHAIRPERSON who was acting as CEO in the wake of Hadebe's departure, appointed Advocate Eric Mkhawane to oversee the grievance hearing and provide a report. Mkhawane made no finding against Oberholzer but recommended better communication between him and Chettiar. In the aftermath of the grievance hearing, Chettiar, with the help of Corruption Watch and the South African Federation of Trade Unions (SAFTU), positioned himself as a victimised whistleblower.[1]

A closer look at the allegations he made, however, does not bear this out, and it will perhaps forever remain unclear why and how he acted when he did. Chettiar passed away in June 2021. I approached his family to ask whether they would be willing to speak with me or share any documents Chettiar may have had in his possession, but I received no response.

During the grievance hearing and immediately afterwards, Chettiar agreed to accept a move out of operations, only to later complain that this was unfair. Oberholzer, meanwhile, acted to suspend him for the false allegations in the grievance. In response, Chettiar filed an unfair labour practice complaint with the Commission for Conciliation, Mediation and Arbitration (CCMA). On 15 March 2020, shortly before the CCMA hearing was due to start, the *Sunday Independent* published an apparently explosive article about Oberholzer's continued shareholding in Stefanutti Stocks – a major contractor to Eskom on the Kusile project. Oberholzer had worked for Stefanutti Stocks between 2009 and 2014 and, as part of his remuneration package, had been given shares in the company, which were held in a First National Bank securities portfolio.[2]

The newspaper, quoting SAFTU's Zwelinzima Vavi calling for Oberholzer to be fired, reported that Oberholzer had met with Stefanutti Stocks on several occasions after taking up his position at Eskom. Eskom confirmed the shareholding, and that Oberholzer had declared this upfront, and revealed that the meetings had taken place in the company of then acting CEO Mabuza. The paper reported that Vavi and Corruption Watch had nevertheless written letters to Eskom, asking for the board to intervene and protect Chettiar, whom they described as a whistleblower.

In late March 2020, Mabuza appointed Advocate Nazeer Cassim to undertake a further investigation into the allegations against Oberholzer, which had morphed slightly since the grievance. Cassim was asked to probe six issues: whether Oberholzer had failed to properly declare his interest in Stefanutti Stocks; whether he had any dealings with the company since his return to Eskom in breach of policy; whether there was any corruption arising from Oberholzer signing a contract with Black & Veatch, as the contract had been modified several times from its original R114-million value in 2006 to over R14 billion in 2020; whether his introduction of disciplinary action against Chettiar constituted victimisation of a whistleblower; the circumstances that led to Chettiar being transferred to another position; and the merits of Chettiar's CCMA complaint alleging unfair labour practice.

Cassim delivered his report on 4 April 2020.[3] He found there was no merit in the complaint regarding corruption around Black & Veatch but recommended further investigation into the nature of the contracts, which appeared to have contravened tender laws.

'There is no factual content supporting allegations of corruption or other wrongful conduct on the part of Oberholzer in relation to his role in the Black and Veatch contract,' Cassim wrote. 'It may be prudent to investigate the particularities justifying the increase from R2.4 billion to R14 billion since 2008 to the present time.'

Cassim found that Oberholzer's shares in Stefanutti Stocks had been allocated to him in 2014, and at the time were worth R600 000. Five years later, when he returned to Eskom, they were worth just over R100 000. At the time of writing the report, they were worth around R6 000. Cassim was satisfied that Oberholzer had appropriately declared the shareholding. But this was only one part of the complaint – Cassim examined minutes of meetings and submissions to the executive tender committee, showing that Oberholzer had signed off on three submissions to the committee that related to Eskom contracts with Stefanutti Stocks.

'In my view whilst, technically speaking, Oberholzer breached the provisions of the Eskom policy – he should have abstained from the transactions in totality – this is not a matter in which he should face a disciplinary hearing,' Cassim wrote in his report. 'First, the matters he engaged in were of an operational nature falling squarely within his responsibilities. Secondly, the contents of the motivations are in the interests of Eskom. Nevertheless, rules must be conformed to. I propose and recommend that the CEO or a nominated board member counsels Oberholzer on the matter.'

What Cassim was unaware of, or could not disclose in his report, was that in August 2018, just weeks after returning to Eskom, Oberholzer had approved a mandate for Bowmans to probe several key contractors at Medupi and Kusile – and of the six issues mentioned for immediate priority, two were contracts with Stefanutti Stocks at Kusile. Oberholzer did not divest his shares, despite knowing what was coming. Instead, he held onto them even as their value dropped from more than R100 000 to less than R6 000.

Cassim was scathing of Chettiar's disclosures to the Zondo Commission and his subsequent claims of being a whistleblower.

'In my view, the COO [Oberholzer] was distraught and emotionally affected by the allegations of dishonesty that he exercised his prerogative to formulate a charge sheet against Chettiar based on the false allegations Chettiar made against him. This action was regrettable,' Cassim found. 'Both actions were unfortunate. Chettiar had no business to report the matter to the Zondo Commission and the COO had no business to charge him for having done so. The reason being that both laboured under the wrong belief that they were doing the right thing. Although both of them believed subjectively that they were doing the right thing, objectively viewed, Chettiar was furthering his own interest because he felt that Oberholzer had undermined him in relation to the Aveng transaction. However, he went overboard in making allegations concerning the honesty of the COO. Similarly, the COO acted hastily and emotionally in bringing the disciplinary charges against Chettiar. He too, overreacted.'

Cassim took it a step further, however, and recommended that Oberholzer face a disciplinary hearing to fully ventilate the issues around the Aveng payment in the interests of 'transparency, accountability and fair play'. In a supplementary report filed with Eskom in June 2020, Cassim backtracked slightly, saying any disciplinary action should be deferred until after the High Court had delivered judgment on Aveng's application to force Eskom to pay the R40 million.

The court eventually ruled in Aveng's favour in a judgment delivered in September 2020, vindicating Möller and Oberholzer, even after Eskom had opposed the application. But, because of the non-payment, Aveng filed R18 million in claims indicating that Eskom had repudiated the contract. They were awarded these claims.

All told, it cost Oberholzer countless hours to deal with Chettiar's grievance and the subsequent investigation by Cassim.

It cost Eskom more than R90 million to resolve the R129 million in claims filed by Aveng in 2018. Of that, R28 million was for legal costs.[4]

The indirect costs to Eskom of having to appoint a new contractor to finish the project initially started by Aveng and for the more than 1 000 trucks a day needed to deliver coal to the power station are yet to be fully quantified. It is estimated, however, to be in the hundreds of millions.

Before the court judgment that vindicated him, Oberholzer would face further investigations, based on the same allegations examined by the commission's investigators and probed by Cassim. Within two years of the Zondo Commission handing its 'report' to Eskom, Oberholzer was investigated five times and cleared on each occasion.

Amid all the chaos, in December 2019, the Majuba rail project was dealt another blow when a fire broke out on a conveyor that transported coal from the stockyard to bunkers closer to the power station. Eskom confirmed to News24 that valves controlling the water supply to the fire-suppression system on the conveyor had been shut off some time prior to the fire breaking out.[5]

It could find no record of a work order that would have required the valves to be closed.

6

Further investigations

ON 27 JULY 2020, PUBLIC ENTERPRISES minister Pravin Gordhan wrote to the Eskom board requesting an investigation into 'allegations of victimisation, nepotism and corruption made against the Chief Operations Officer by an alleged whistleblower, Mark Chettiar'.[1]

Gordhan told the board that trade union body SAFTU had brought the allegations to his attention. He also asked the board to investigate Oberholzer's alleged failure to declare his shareholding in Stefanutti Stocks, the significant increases in the value of the Black & Veatch contract, and the role played by Oberholzer in the Aveng matter. He indicated his agreement with Cassim's recommendation that Eskom await the outcome of the High Court application brought by Aveng before instituting disciplinary action.

André de Ruyter, in his capacity as chief executive officer, was tasked to investigate the issues and report back to the board so that it could make a decision on whether or not to take disciplinary action against Oberholzer. De Ruyter provided his report to the board a little under a month later, on 24 August 2020.

The first issue covered in his report was Oberholzer's shareholding in Stefanutti Stocks.

'The COO wrote a letter on 8 August 2019, 23 days after joining Eskom, to Bowmans Forensic Investigators requesting them to pay specific attention to Stefanutti Stocks as one of the contractors alleged to have colluded with Eskom officials and defrauded Eskom of ... millions,' De Ruyter wrote. 'It can be argued that if the COO had acted to protect his own financial interests, he would have sold his shares at the time with the information at his disposal and not have waited until the shares had effectively no value.'

He set out how, when Oberholzer joined Eskom, the shares were valued at just over R103 000. When Oberholzer finally sold the shares on 30 March 2020, he received, after brokerage fees, R2 894.60, which he donated to his church.

'The fact that he had owned the shares, declared his interest, and then acted without any regard for the personal financial consequences to him of his actions appears to be an adequate rebuttal of allegations that he pursued his own agenda at the expense of Eskom in order to generate a financial benefit for himself,' De Ruyter found. He added that Oberholzer had been subjected to a lifestyle audit, which revealed no areas of concern.

He then moved on to Oberholzer's meetings with Stefanutti Stocks. He had confirmed that Oberholzer had not worked on any Eskom/Kusile contracts during or after his employment with Stefanutti Stocks. De Ruyter explained in his report that, after his return to Eskom, Oberholzer had two meetings with Stefanutti managing director Russell Crawford.

At the first meeting, Oberholzer was accompanied by Jabu Mabuza as acting CEO and chairperson, legal heads Bartlett Hewu and Jerome Mthembu, as well as Binesh Singh, the projects director for Kusile at the time. Singh was again present at the second meeting and was joined by Avin Maharaj, another senior management official responsible for Kusile and who would subsequently replace Singh as projects director. Stefanutti Stocks commercial director John le Riche was also present at this second meeting.

Oberholzer co-signed two modifications to a contract that Stefanutti Stocks had in conjunction with Basil Read, for the construction of dozens of miscellaneous buildings at Kusile. The other signatory was Solly Tshitangano, Eskom's chief procurement officer (CPO). The first modification was for a 14-month time extension, due to site access delays. The second was for a R268-million increase in contract value, due to increases in quantities, design changes, late access claims and other allowances. This submission went to the board's investment and finance committee, then to the board, after which approval had to be obtained from National Treasury.

'Eskom governance processes do not allow any one individual to approve contract modifications, there is a very structured process ensuring the necessary approval. The COO co-signed the submissions in his capacity as acting group chief executive for group capital also responsible for the Kusile power station project. The Kusile Projects Director and his team and not Oberholzer motivated at the relevant governance structures for approval,' De Ruyter found, noting that Oberholzer had worked closely with forensic investigators from Bowmans as well as the SIU.

He next tackled the Aveng issue to some extent.

'It is clear that the alleged whistleblower was an instrumental part of the process from inception to the point of supporting and preparing the relevant documents for approval of the proposed payment to Aveng,' De Ruyter noted. 'It is also clearly evident that the COO did not propose payment of R40 million to Aveng. Rather, the COO ensured that due process according to Eskom requirements was followed, independent legal advice was obtained ... and only when the matter was raised by the Zondo Commission, was the payment stopped as a precautionary measure.'

De Ruyter recommended that the board should not institute disciplinary action against Oberholzer, adding that it was apparent that an underperforming employee, Chettiar, had sought to portray himself as a whistleblower when Oberholzer tried to hold him accountable for poor performance 'presumably to prolong the period of his employment ... The alleged whistleblower has in the process inflicted substantial reputational damage on the COO, with his allegations not corroborated by the facts or evidence.'

In conclusion, De Ruyter wrote: 'The present report is the third investigation into the alleged actions of the COO as presented by Mr Chettiar. It is recommended that the board endorses the COO's actions as having been fair, transparent, procedural and professional in upholding and fulfilling his contractual mandate in serving the interests of his employer Eskom, and that note is taken of an emerging pattern of underperformers to style themselves as whistleblowers when called to account, a trend that is entirely at odds with the desired high-performance culture that Eskom is seeking to inculcate in its employees.'

When the High Court delivered its judgment two weeks later, Eskom issued a press statement announcing Oberholzer's vindication and that it had adopted De Ruyter's report, which it published. Undeterred, SAFTU approached the Public Protector, hoping to find a more sympathetic audience. But in late 2021, Public Protector Busisiwe Mkhwebane closed the investigation, having found that SAFTU's complaint that Eskom and Gordhan had not properly investigated Chettiar's allegations was baseless.[2]

The fourth issue De Ruyter had been asked to investigate, and for which he cleared Oberholzer of wrongdoing, was the Black & Veatch contract that had ballooned from R2.4 billion to R14 billion during Oberholzer's 10-year hiatus in the private sector. De Ruyter did, however, recommend that the numerous modifications to the contract be probed.

At this point, it is necessary to take another step back.

In 2008, Oberholzer signed a modified contract with Kansas-based engineering firm Black & Veatch to help provide engineers and other specialists needed to build the coal-fired power plants. The original contract for R114 million, signed in 2006, had been initiated in 2005 when Eskom realised it needed engineering expertise on its major new build programmes, as well as the refurbishment of the older stations. Black & Veatch was later appointed the implementation partner on Kusile, while Parsons Brinckerhoff Power Africa (PB Power Africa) was appointed to oversee Medupi. An alliance of two companies – Murray & Roberts and ESBI, an international engineering consultancy based in Ireland – was appointed as a third partner in the roll-out of Eskom's new build programme. Together, they would become known as the Engineering Houses

Panel – effectively, there was a set contract value, and task orders could be issued to any of these three companies to undertake work required by Eskom. It was the first time Eskom had used this model.

Prior to Medupi and Kusile, the companies had worked interchangeably on the construction of Eskom's open cycle gas turbines, as well as its new Ingula pumped storage scheme and the Sere wind farm, the utility's first wind-turbine installation.

Besides the new builds, the panel was also asked to assist Eskom in the return to service of Camden, Grootvlei and Komati power stations, which had been mothballed years before due to excess generation capacity. Additional work was undertaken by the panel at Kriel, Arnot, Matla and Duvha to refurbish the ageing stations and increase their capacity with upgrades – all under the capital expansion programme umbrella.

For all this work, Eskom had an approved contract value of R280 million. By mid-2007, however, 95 per cent of the contact value had already been used up – and the projects were all ongoing. Accordingly, approval was sought and granted for the contracts to be modified and extended for four years with commensurate value increases. By now, Oberholzer was acting head of capital expansion, his predecessor Peter O'Connor having resigned in 2007.

The Black & Veatch contract was modified into two components – named onshore and offshore agreements – for legal and tax reasons, as now some of the design work for Kusile could be undertaken in the US at the company's offices in Kansas. In March 2008, after a protracted negotiation by the commercial team, Oberholzer, as acting head of capital expansion and Eskom's duly appointed employer's agent, signed the onshore and offshore agreements for Black & Veatch to become Eskom's engineering partner on Kusile. Documents show the new contracts were recorded as a restatement of the original 2006 contract. From Eskom's point of view, the modified contract was less risky, as the scope of the work was more clearly defined and guarantees had been obtained from the Black & Veatch parent company covering their local and international activities in terms of the contract. But it was a moot point. Eskom needed their expertise. The power stations had to be built as fast as possible. If government had not delayed and had approved the building of new capacity in the late 1990s, things would have been different.

'I am not saying we wouldn't have made mistakes,' Oberholzer conceded to me. 'But it would have been very different.'[3]

A few months later, in December 2008, Oberholzer left Eskom – the value of the Black & Veatch contract was now R2.4 billion and it was valid until March 2017.

More than a decade later, on 4 March 2020, Oberholzer and his colleagues from Eskom were before Parliament's Standing Committee on Public Accounts (SCOPA) when chief procurement officer Solly Tshitangano showed a slide during his presentation that listed the numerous modifications to the Black & Veatch contract that had occurred over the years. The next slide was a clipped screenshot of Oberholzer's signature on the 2008 contract.

Oberholzer was blindsided. There had been no mention of this during the preparation meeting the day before, when the delegation had met and run through the presentations to prepare for any questions that might come up.

The Black & Veatch contract had been modified on six occasions, for time and value, and today stood at just over R14 billion, with a significant portion of expenditure on Kusile. Tshitangano seemed to be implying that Oberholzer was responsible for approving the increase from the original R114 million to R14 billion. But Oberholzer had not even been at Eskom when most of these modifications took place.

This allegation formed part of Cassim's and De Ruyter's subsequent probes, both of which cleared Oberholzer of any wrongdoing. Apparently dissatisfied with their findings, Tshitangano mandated Eskom's internal audit and forensics department to undertake its own preliminary review of the contract, and forensic firm Crawford Independent Associate was subsequently appointed to investigate further. In 2019, Crawford had been appointed to a panel of forensic investigators that would be utilised by Eskom for the next five years.

It is worth noting that, at this point, forensic probes undertaken by Bowmans at Kusile had already unearthed major corruption schemes involving the inflating of claims and contract values in exchange for kickbacks. The Black & Veatch contract for Kusile encompassed not only designing the power station but also providing on-the-ground engineering support throughout its construction. Black & Veatch engineers are still present at Kusile today.

On the face of it, it seemed logical that the contract had to be extended numerous times over the years, as Kusile was beset with delays caused by a host of reasons. Eskom also did not have any in-house expertise in building power stations, and so Black & Veatch's services could be considered invaluable.

It therefore came as a surprise when Crawford delivered their draft report in March 2021.[4] In the main, their findings were against Oberholzer, largely ignoring the processes and rationale behind the five further modifications that had increased the contract value by some R12 billion. They recommended that Eskom consider disciplinary action against Oberholzer for signing the 2008 contract, which, they said, amounted to irregular expenditure – this, 13 years after the fact. Crawford further reasoned that because the modified contract was irregular, all subsequent modifications were also irregular, but they provided no in-depth analysis of the motivations or approvals for the five other modifications.

The report is, at its core, contradictory. It found that approval processes were not followed regarding the delegation of consent forms relating to four contract modifications between 2010 and 2016. It deemed these modifications irregular expenditure amounting to R9.7 billion and alleged that Oberholzer may have breached provisions of the Public Finance Management Act by failing to ensure there was no irregular expenditure. Yet these modifications were made during Oberholzer's time away from Eskom.

Furthermore, Crawford found that Oberholzer should never have signed the 2008 contracts because, despite being the appointed employer's agent, he was also the acting manager for the capital expansion programme responsible for executing the new build programme and did not have the authority to sign them. According to Crawford, he should have 'transferred' the employer's agent component of his responsibilities while he was acting manager for capital expansion to someone else, 'before signing the 2008 Black and Veatch contracts'. This, even though as head of capital expansion Oberholzer had the required delegation of authority to implement a contract that had been negotiated by the commercial division, which was not under his control.

The most striking aspect of the report, however, is that Crawford made recommendations for disciplinary action against Oberholzer only, and not any of the many other Eskom officials involved at the time and who were still at the utility.

Oberholzer was incensed. He put together a report of his own, detailing the shortcomings of the Crawford report.[5] He described how, on 2 March 2021, Crawford had interviewed him in the presence of an audit and forensics department employee.

'The questions posed to me were very general in nature including a couple of questions on the onshore and offshore agreements, and nothing specific centred on any possible deviation,' Oberholzer wrote in his report, dated 16 June 2021. 'I was asked if I believed I had the delegation of authority to sign these agreements, and I answered in the affirmative.'

According to Oberholzer, he informed Crawford's investigators that the commercial team at the time had been the custodians of the agreements.

'It was the first time in 13 years that these issues were raised and I was receptive and welcomed the opportunity for the interview and to share the facts of my involvement with the contract,' he continued. 'My responses were off the cuff and to the best of my knowledge, having to reflect back 16 years ago to when the original contract was signed in 2006.'

The draft report landed just days after this meeting. Oberholzer was taken aback and immediately asked for a further meeting to present his side of the story in more detail. In this meeting, held on 13 May 2021, Oberholzer handed over a thick lever arch file with hundreds of pages of documentary evidence to support his version of events. Despite this, Crawford stood by its draft findings and provided a final report to Eskom on 28 May.

Oberholzer set about conducting interviews, contacting individuals who had been at Eskom at the time, and gathering documents that Crawford and Eskom's own audit and forensics department claimed they could not find. Several officials who had been part of managing the Black & Veatch contract over the years also objected to Crawford's characterisation of irregular expenditure.

'It must be noted that both [audit and forensics] and Crawford were negligent in that they overlooked key, salient points by not adequately investigating nor addressing procurement's accountability as custodians of the proceed to conclude if due diligence and governance protocols were indeed followed and implemented within procurement,' he wrote in his June 2021 report. 'The question that needs to be asked, is why would an external independent investigating house be reticent and not open and receptive to the facts presented – is there another agenda?'

Oberholzer provided his view on the contracts with Black & Veatch succinctly: 'The crux of the matter is that the onshore and offshore agreements were a restatement, supplementing the original signed contract, giving effect to the approved modification by the board tender committee on 5 September 2007, cognisant of the [committee's] resolution endorsed in December 2005 to [capital expansion]. Also very important is to note that there was no change to the contract conditions, no increase in risk (there was actually a reduction) and both Black and Veatch entities were (and are) jointly and severally liable.'

Crucially, Crawford found no evidence of corruption. After extensively probing contracts at Kusile, I too have found no indication to suggest corruption on the part of Black & Veatch or Oberholzer. This would almost certainly have come to light at this late juncture, considering the length and value of the contract. Not one Eskom official has given any indication that the Black & Veatch contract could be lumped together with those Kusile contracts where corruption was rife.

In any event, if Crawford is proved correct that the R9.7 billion in modifications was indeed irregular expenditure, the logical question that must then be asked is whether there was value for money. How do you quantify this in the context of a project like Kusile? Does the country need the power station? Yes. Were there many delays? Yes. Is Black & Veatch to blame for the design flaws? No. They did not force Eskom to choose supercritical boilers for Kusile and Medupi, a decision that, considering the design flaws and the fact that the utility had zero experience in running, building or maintaining these types of boilers, was apparently suicidal.

These are all factors that will have to be considered when Eskom applies for condonation of the supposed irregular expenditure, which is by no means an indication of corruption. It merely means one of a plethora of procurement hoops was not jumped through to the satisfaction of onlookers more than a decade after the fact.

'It is very disconcerting that 14 years later the delegation of authority and my integrity is questioned, despite the facts, including affidavits of key personnel who were involved with this project and who are still working for Eskom,' Oberholzer wrote.

Tellingly, Tshitangano had requested investigations into not only Black & Veatch but also PB Power Africa and ESBI/Murray & Roberts, the other two engineering houses on the panel.

'We are yet to see a report on the investigation outcome on PB Africa and ESBI/Murray and Roberts, which raises a lot of questions on the intent of the CPO as he was also responsible for raising the Black and Veatch contract modifications issue at SCOPA on 4 March 2020,' Oberholzer noted. '[I]s it perhaps because it is the only area where Jan Oberholzer's signature appears?'

A closer look at Crawford gives rise to further concerns. According to company records and publicly available information, Crawford is registered as Chedza International Loss Adjusters. It seems that around 2009, Chedza purchased Crawford & Company South Africa from its international parent company, US-based Crawford & Company, and changed the name to Crawford Independent Associate.

Chedza was founded by noted black business pioneer Professor Mohale Mahanyele and is today run by one of his daughters, Mpho Mahanyele. On its website, Chedza records that 'the future of Chedza International is navigated by Mpho Mahanyele and the Mahanyele family whose powerful woman [sic] are committed to continuing their father's legacy'.[6]

Mpho's sister, Phuthi Mahanyele, is the CEO of Naspers South Africa, the first black woman to ever hold this position. Information on Chedza's website implies she is involved in the company's affairs, but company records show she has never been a director. This in itself is not problematic. It is normal for businesses to pass to family members. What is unusual, however, is that Phuthi is married to Sifiso Dabengwa, the former chief executive of the MTN Group and a former Eskom board member. Seen as a close ally of President Cyril Ramaphosa, Dabengwa was one of the trustees of the Ria Tenda Trust, established as a vehicle to house funds donated to Ramaphosa's CR17 campaign for the ANC presidency.

At the time Crawford was appointed to Eskom's panel of forensic investigators in 2019, Dabengwa was still an Eskom board member. (He resigned in July 2020.)

Eskom told me that Crawford had not declared any conflict of interest during the bidding process, and when asked in a follow-up question seeking clarity on whether the utility was of the view that Crawford should have done so, Eskom said yes, it should have.

'Crawford did not comply with the declaration of conflict requirement which is to complete the Eskom Conflict of Interest form. This form is standard and requires declaration of interest in instances where such interest is vested upon or relates to an Eskom employee/contractor/consultant/director involved in the tender evaluation/tender adjudication/tender negotiation,' the utility said in an emailed response on 17 March 2022.

Dabengwa, for his part, denied any knowledge of the company being appointed to work at Eskom.

Mpho and Phuthi were both approached for comment. Mpho responded saying that she had sent my questions on to Eskom and was awaiting the utility's response before she could comment. Phuthi never replied.

Despite Crawford's recommendations and Eskom confirming that it had considered the report, Oberholzer has never been disciplined. Seemingly, the utility decided not to act on what could be construed as a dubious attempt to get Oberholzer fired.

It was not, however, the end of the line for Chettiar's allegations. In April 2021, the SIU confirmed to News24 that it had instituted an investigation into Eskom's COO 'on the basis of allegations made regarding Mr Oberholzer in the media and during SIU and Eskom presentations to Scopa'.[7] According to sources, the probe was at Oberholzer's request and had his 'full blessing', although the SIU claimed the decision to investigate was based on allegations in the public domain. Whatever the case, 'Mr Oberholzer offered to co-operate with the SIU's investigation, including voluntarily making his bank statements available to the SIU for review,' SIU spokesperson Kaizer Kganyago told News24 at the time. Indeed, it would be the most in-depth and invasive investigation into Oberholzer thus far and included forensic analyses of both his and his wife Lindy's bank accounts.

On 31 August 2021, News24 confirmed with the SIU that it too had cleared Oberholzer of wrongdoing 'in a sweeping probe, spanning 12 months, that covered allegations of nepotism, corruption, maladministration and conflicts of interest'.[8] It was clear from the documents that Oberholzer submitted in response to the Crawford report that the Black & Veatch issue had formed part of the SIU probe.

Tshitangano's motivation for going after Oberholzer remains unclear. He maintained in written responses to my questions that the Crawford probe was negatively impacted because he was suspended and later fired before he could submit an affidavit to investigators.[9] I can only speculate that he was pre-empting rumours that Oberholzer was about to remove him for poor performance – which he also denies.

'I really did not expect any other outcome,' Oberholzer told News24 about the SIU's findings. 'Being justly vindicated after five intense investigations with the same outcome, my integrity and value system remains resolute and support that the truth be publicly known. However, I am not naive. It is inevitable that there will be more allegations and malicious attacks, which are only to be expected as I am dealing decisively with corruption, maladministration, incompetence and poor performance.'

7

The new captain

ANDRÉ DE RUYTER ARRIVED AT Eskom in early 2020 to take up what many have called the toughest job in South Africa. He started days before he was meant to, as a load-shedding crisis enveloped the power utility and he hoped to get stuck in as quickly as possible.

His appointment had been announced in late 2019 to general incredulity from some corners, as his name had not featured in the intense media and industry speculation over Hadebe's possible successors. The unions, particularly the NUM, condemned the appointment of a white CEO as a blow to transformation, while the Economic Freedom Fighters (EFF) said it was part of a racist project by Gordhan to undermine capable African professionals.[1]

De Ruyter was also joining Eskom after four years as CEO of Nampak, and critics quickly pointed to the company's disastrous share-price collapse during his tenure as a sign of bad things to come for the country – ignoring the facts of what had occurred at Nampak.

In January 2020, the *Financial Mail* quoted Peter Attard Montalto of Intellidex saying scathingly that De Ruyter was a 'compromise candidate' and that he lacked 'the level of self-confident leadership that is required to hold your own against an undercapacitated board and with an interventionist shareholder. This is not a positive; as such we struggle to see it [De Ruyter's appointment] really meets the credibility bar.'[2]

Perhaps predictably, De Ruyter would be accused of racism a year later by an underperforming executive, chief procurement officer Solly Tshitangano, which the unions and the EFF apparently had no trouble believing despite ample evidence to the contrary.

What few could have predicted was the determination with which De Ruyter has stood his ground. Despite continued criticism over Eskom's inability to curb load shedding, which is the worst it has ever been, and despite near unprecedented and repeated attacks designed to discredit and remove him from office, he has remained steadfast.

'Unfortunately, or fortunately, I quite like a good fight,' he told me during our interview in January 2022. 'I also like robust intellectual engagement. But, if you write bullshit to me ... I will respond. I guess you could call it a fuck-you attitude. Take me on with something I have done wrong, and I will accept it. But don't come with a spurious argument that doesn't hold water. I will respond to it.'[3]

True to his word, De Ruyter has not only weathered the storm of attacks and allegations, but his accusers, including Tshitangano and a board member, are no longer at Eskom, Tshitangano having been taken to task for his actions and the board member shown to have made apparently false claims.

At six foot five, De Ruyter towers over almost everyone in the room. He is obviously fit and starts most days with a session in the gym. The youngest of four siblings, he was born in Pretoria in 1968, but the family relocated to Bronkhorstspruit while he was still young. Now in his early fifties, the only clue to his age is his completely grey hair. He laughs easily when recalling lighter moments from his past, but switches smoothly to a more serious and intense tone when speaking about Eskom's challenges.

His father, who passed away in 2006, was an engineering technician for Bruinette Kruger Stoffberg (BKS), one of the country's oldest engineering consulting firms. His mother, who is 84 and living in the Western Cape, was a nurse at an old-age home in Bronkhorstspruit.

De Ruyter describes his childhood as carefree.

'I was barefoot, with shorts and a T-shirt and my bicycle, and off I would go,' he laughed. 'To this day there is a certain type of South African Englishman who will ask you where you went to school, as if it's relevant, and then I will say with some mischievous delight, Bronkhorstspruit!'

THE NEW CAPTAIN

Later, the family returned to Pretoria, and De Ruyter finished high school at Menlo Park before enrolling at the University of Pretoria for a bachelor's in English and psychology.

'I was always obsessed with English literature, I still am,' he explained.

Later he would add law as a subject and complete two degrees simultaneously.

'The beauty of the billing system at UP was that you could add as many subjects as you liked and not pay more tuition. I knew even then that a degree in English literature was not going to pay the bills.'

De Ruyter worked three jobs during university to pay for his studies.

'My father, a staunch Calvinist, said, okay, you want to go and study, I will pay for your books but the rest you have to sort out yourself,' he said.

So two nights a week he drove a Volkswagen Golf around the city as a courier for a pathologist and had a small business proofreading theses for 'mainly engineering students who couldn't write that well'. On Fridays and Saturdays, he worked as a barman at the Pretoria Country Club, which was where he met his wife.

'Her mother was horrified, and wanted to make sure that I was in fact a student and not a professional barman,' he laughed. 'That was that. Three years, and then when I graduated with my BA I got a permanent job at one of the places where I worked a holiday job as a student, a joint venture between BKS and PB Steyn, which was known as Tolplan. There I learned the fine art of writing cabinet memoranda and submissions to the minister, "attached please find for your signature should you concur with the contents thereof", you know, honourable minister kind of thing.'

At the same time, he completed a bachelor's degree in civil law and recalls vividly how, one afternoon on his way to evening classes on his motorbike, he was caught in a Pretoria thunderstorm.

'I remember how my soaking wet office shoes squelched as I walked into the class,' he laughed. 'I worked there for four years, and then I got lucky. I was already committed to do national service and then they reduced it from two years to one year.'

De Ruyter did his basic training in Bethlehem and then, surprisingly, opted to join the police when they came to recruit.

'When I look back on it now, I never had much of a youth, to be honest; I just worked my arse off. I started formal work at 21, having finished high school at 17. I think it's the Protestant work ethic – your future is in your hands and you know, you have to work.'

Soon after arriving at Maleoskop, a training ground for police recruits that resembles a military training camp but with, according to De Ruyter, far more food, 'they figured out that I needed to be in the police language services'.

After completing national service through 1990 and 1991, he returned to Tolplan.

'One day, I saw an advertisement in the newspaper for a commercial advisor at a coal giant, and I thought it must be Eskom – but it turned out to be Sasol when I went for the interview.'

In 1993, De Ruyter got married and moved to Secunda to take up his first job with Sasol, where he would remain for the next two decades. In the early years of his time at Sasol, De Ruyter also completed an LLB degree through the University of South Africa (UNISA) and recalls how on some evenings his wife, a community planner, would run meetings about proposed projects and he would sit and complete his UNISA assignments.

'I saw the sun set and rise in my office at Secunda a couple of times, and it was just, that's what you did, and that was hard work,' he said. 'But I did make a nuisance of myself because I always said that I wanted to travel, always had the travel bug ever since I read a book, *Het leven van een landloper* by A. den Doolaard, which was about a Dutchman who also worked in an office who said one day he was going to become a vagrant.'

His nagging worked.

'I was appointed to be the commercial officer on the Oosdraai coal-export plant, where I learned a lot about projects, and coal quality ... A lot of what I learned about coal I learned there,' he said. 'After that, I was promoted to a very important title – assistant marketing manager for coal exports – and then I moved to Rosebank to the head office and it was all very fancy. I even had my own office.'

Having made it sufficiently clear that he wanted to travel, De Ruyter was then asked to sell coal internationally, where he worked with Rob Turner.

'It was a privilege to work with Rob, a fantastic guy who was highly experienced in business, and we sold coal internationally. Rob was significantly shorter than I am, so the joke was always that we were the long and the short of coal marketing,' De Ruyter laughed. 'One of the things I will always remember about Rob during our travels is that Japan is a very civilised culture, Korea is a very aggressive, abrasive culture and you could see how on the flight from Japan to Korea, how he would change gears in his head and become aggressive, so that he could move from this polite person kind of thing, so that cultural adaptability, that was very interesting to see.'

Of his travels, De Ruyter said: 'I learned huge amounts. I mean, I went to Brazil, to the steel mills in places called Belo Horizonte, Vitória, places no tourist ever goes to. And you just learn. I wrote all the contracts, that's what I did, and I guess I could speak reasonably well. That helped.'

At the time, Sasol was targeting Japan's steel industry as its primary market, and De Ruyter recalls an incident when he decided to teach a group of visiting Japanese businessmen a few Afrikaans phrases on a game drive during which the game proved shy.

'On the last night, Chris Cloete, who was the MD of Sasol Mining at the time, gave a big speech and he duly trotted out some of his Japanese phrases, you know, *Domo arigato gozaimasu*, thank you very, very much. And you know, the leader of the Japanese delegation stood up and said in very accented Afrikaans, *Dis 'n moerse plesier!*'

On another occasion, Turner and De Ruyter found themselves upgraded to a suite at the London Hilton hotel after a gruelling sales trip that had taken them from Japan to Korea, Taiwan and Spain. Surveying the suite, De Ruyter said he felt he had 'arrived'.

'So we explored the contents of the minibar for a moment before we went out for dinner, you know, we were in a good mood. And the lifts open for us to go down and it's filled with, you know, we called them penguins, these very stiff-upper-lip Brits with the whole bow tie and tails, and I said, no, you can go down, but Rob being quite small and aggressive said, no, come in, you know, there's space, and he sort of forced his way in. So I went in but there was no room for me to do the polite thing and turn around and look at the numbers, so I faced all of them. And being somewhat taller than the average Brit, I immediately had eye contact with all of them so I felt compelled to say the first thing that came into my mind, which was, "You are probably wondering why I called this meeting!"'

The gentlemen in the lift that night did not laugh. But, said De Ruyter, 'you have to have fun. I think that's what Rob also taught me, you have to have fun. When it's not fun any more, it becomes a burden.'

At 29, De Ruyter's travel bug caused him to seize with two hands an opportunity to study for an MBA at Nyenrode Business University in the Netherlands when a professor who had overseen a short course introduced him to Bas Kardol, one of the founders of Investec.

'I then get called for an interview with Mr Kardol to see if he can give me a bursary. So, I go to his little *pied-à-terre* in Rosebank, and get introduced to him and his wife and we make small talk while his wife goes to make coffee in the kitchen,' he recalled. 'As his wife enters with the tray, like a good Afrikaans boy, I jumped up to collect the tray from her, and I mean that's what you do. It's good manners. And he looks at me and looks at his wife and says, *Moeder, ik denk dat we in deze jongeman een beurs landen geheffen.* So good manners do pay off.'

His wife and nine-month-old daughter accompanied him to the Netherlands, where they lived in a small apartment on the campus.

'It was a fantastic experience – we had absolutely bugger all. When we had a party, you went with your own plate and cutlery because no one had more than one of each, that's just how it worked. We were something like 56 students from 22 nationalities, Americans, Cubans and Russians, Germans and Dutch, of course.'

Obtaining his MBA, he said, proved pivotal in his later career.

After a year at Nyenrode, De Ruyter returned to South Africa and worked on a natural gas project in Mozambique.

'I negotiated the shareholders' agreement and came up with an innovative concept that essentially had convertible preferred shares for the government, you know, complicated stories. But I think that got me under the attention of some senior people at Sasol.'

He was quickly pulled into Sasol's group strategy division, where he worked closely with Pat Davies, the then CEO. He describes Davies as someone who possesses 'huge personal integrity' and who was a key influence on his career.

'He was really a fantastic person to work with – very dedicated, very committed and very hard working but always about the principle. At that time Sasol had its issues with the Competition Commission, but he would always stick to the principle, do what's right and come clean, don't try and sweep things under the rug. That experience was really valuable for me,' De Ruyter said. 'From there I went to Sasol Oil as head of strategy and planning, and that got me into a lot of contact with the government because the oil industry is heavily regulated, so I spent a lot of time in Pretoria talking to the department of mineral resources and energy.'

It was during this time that he first met Rod Crompton, who was a deputy director general at the time. Crompton serves on the Eskom board and was a familiar face when De Ruyter arrived. At the time, he also met Nhlanhla Gumede, now a full-time regulator at the National Energy Regulator of South Africa with which Eskom is engaged in running battles over tariffs. Nelisiwe Magubane, formerly a deputy director general with the department of public enterprises, is also a board member and similarly has interacted with De Ruyter in the past.

'We had travelled to Singapore together as part of a GIBS Business

School course Sasol had put on,' he explained. 'There was a bit of history there, and a bit of a network there. And I guess the message is to be good and polite to all people at all times because you never know when they will play an important role in your life going forward.'

This would prove crucial later, he said, when he was accused of racism – some board members had at least interacted with him in the past and knew his disposition.

In 2007, De Ruyter was sent to manage a project in China for Sasol where he experienced huge personal enrichment, but business, he said, was very tough.

'I compared it to trench warfare, you know, you lob a grenade over and wait for the response,' he laughed.

As soon as he arrived in China, he undertook a new prefeasibility study and said he quickly realised that the project was dead in the water. He then had to approach the Sasol executive committee and tell them as much. Their response was that he needed to try harder.

'There were some really, really hard negotiations. But also tough because I had to tell all the project team I had established, the spouses, you know, I called them in and had to tell them, look it's going really badly with the project, please understand that we may have to relocate you so all your Chinese lessons and things you are doing may not last so long,' De Ruyter recalled. 'But open communications, I think that was one of the best things I learned. Kill the rumours by being honest. I had realised that China was never going to happen. Afterward Sasol spent another R1 billion and another year trying to make the project work and only then said, okay, we don't have a project. That gave me faith in my judgement – that I tend to see the answer more quickly than most.'

After nearly a year in China, De Ruyter again relocated his family – by then his two sons had been born – this time to Germany. Some years previously, Sasol had bought a German business, Condea, which it renamed Sasol Olefins and Surfactants (O&S).

'This was when every South African company went abroad to buy businesses in Europe and I think the Germans saw us coming,' De Ruyter told me.

O&S performed so poorly that Sasol had decided to sell it, but the best offer they had received was less than the value of the inventory the company had in storage and was gross of environmental liability, meaning Sasol would probably have had to pay a significant sum of money to get rid of the sprawling business.

'So the decision was taken to try and turn around the business, it was sort of a final roll of the dice. So I phoned Davies, who I then knew, and said I would like to have a go at being part of the team. And he agreed.'

De Ruyter was appointed as leader of the turnaround team, working with Hannes Botha and Dr Johan Botha (no relation), 'a very intelligent character' with whom he remains friends. When Hannes Botha returned to South Africa, De Ruyter became the managing director, overseeing operations in Germany, the US, Italy, Dubai, China and the Czech Republic.

'It was a huge, huge experience going to the plants and talking to people. People are fundamentally good everywhere, that was my observation. I am very much a Theory Y type of person. I tend to assume good faith, and that is being eroded at the moment,' he said.

By the time he left O&S, it was the second-most profitable business operated by Sasol.

'Looking back to when I was appointed by Eskom, I totally underplayed my experience in coal, and my business turnaround experience, as well as learning to work in multicultural environments with different technologies where I could immerse myself in the detail,' De Ruyter said.

He recalls he once sent Dr Botha an email about the hardness of water and how that impacts on 'the surfactants formulation for detergents'. And Botha wrote back and said: *'Jy moet net sê as jy my fokken werk wil doen, dan kan jy R&D kom operate.'* (You must just tell me if you want to come and do my job, then you can come and run research and development.)

De Ruyter ascribes an inherent curiosity, which he satiates by asking questions, wanting to understand the why of things, with helping him gain valuable understanding of how things work. 'Why does this work, why doesn't that work, why is this technology like this, is there a better way, is there another way?'

Former colleagues told the *Financial Mail* that De Ruyter would often be spotted at work on the weekends, speaking to workers on all levels of the business. The publication also described a video De Ruyter had submitted as part of his application for the Eskom job, which included shots of his work boots, well-worn and dusty from years spent traversing the incline shafts and plants at Sasol.[4]

But he also learned the importance of client relationships.

'Very few people in government, also in SOEs, have sat across [from] a customer who doesn't want to buy your product, who says actually I am not interested in you. I don't like you, I don't like your products, I think your prices are excessive, so what are we talking about?' he explained to me.[5]

After Germany, De Ruyter returned to South Africa where he essentially was asked to oversee most of Sasol's operations – including in Secunda, Sasolburg and the company's chemical operations. When Canadian David Constable was appointed as Sasol CEO after Davies's departure, he was asked to look after the chemical operations only. De Ruyter wouldn't be drawn into talking about reports that relations between him and Constable were fractious. He was well placed to secure the top job at Sasol in a few more years, to which he responded only with 'maybe'.

'I was not comfortable at Sasol any more. You want to be able to do a job where you feel that you can make a contribution. The politics became very unpleasant, very stressful, and I wasn't up for that,' he said.

It was at this time, 2014, that De Ruyter got a call from a headhunter. The job on offer was at Nampak, and considering his unhappiness at Sasol, he decided to accept the interview and later the job when it was offered to him. But Nampak, the country's largest packaging company, would prove difficult for De Ruyter.

'I didn't do my due diligence on the gearing of the company,' he told me. 'So the mistake I made at Nampak, I should have very early on done a rights issue to bring down the debt. The company had, in fact, after I had already accepted the position, the then incumbent CEO Andrew Marshall completed an acquisition of a beverage can plant in Nigeria for $300 million and overpaid by about $200 million, which was then subsequently written off as goodwill. I mean, $200 million is a lot of money for any company. And the debt of course was in dollars, and then the flow of the dollars stopped because of the collapse of the oil price, this was in 2015/16. The major projects we pursued in Nigeria and Angola that ramped up the gearing were in countries that had exposure to the oil price and where liquidity and the ability to expatriate profits then became impossible.'

As a result, Nampak's share price took a major hit – a total of 81 per cent over the four years De Ruyter was CEO. The company had to continue to pay its large debts in dollars, with an increasingly weakening rand currency. At the time Nampak decided to venture into Africa, the market had applauded, De Ruyter explained.

'It was like when all South African companies were going into Europe and Sasol bought Condea, the same thing happened to Nampak. Nampak went into Africa when that was the flavour *du jour*, and everybody said yes, and the share price ramped up and you know, there was this thing of exposure to a billion sub-Saharan customers. But then reality set in and gravity reasserted itself and, you know, the share price collapsed. So that was tough, it was difficult. Nampak's performance during my tenure as a CEO was disappointing. There's no two ways about that. I think my [chief financial officer] Glenn Fullerton and I did whatever we could and I honestly think we worked minor miracles to persuade the banks, to keep them onboard, to improve the business, to renegotiate contracts, and again with my O&S experience, focus on safety, operational excellence, working capital, margins.'

Nampak expanded its glass manufacturing business during his tenure, which did not perform poorly, but which, according to De Ruyter, was obscured with the liquidity challenges in Nigeria and Angola.

'In retrospect you know that was a hospital pass. With hindsight I should have seen it coming, so I will accept the blame that I didn't appreciate the strategic risk of taking on a dollar loan, to be repaid from a country with huge exposure to a dollar-denominated commodity. And when that country's economy goes south, your ability to repay goes south as well. But in fairness, a former governor of the Reserve Bank was the chairman of the board when these projects were approved,' he added, referring to Tito Mboweni, who would later serve as finance minister. 'And I think there was sound thinking. It was a black swan event, and that black swan happened and then of course I had to do some very unpopular things, you know, cut the dividend for the first time in something like 32 years. There were analysts that were hugely upset with me.'

But, he added, the analyst community also needed to shoulder some of the blame for Nampak's decline.

'My predecessor as I understand it got a huge amount of pressure from the investment community, ironically for Nampak having a lazy balance sheet. It's undergeared, where is your growth, you are not doing anything, and then what did he do? He went out and said, okay you fuckers, I will show you, and I will go and grow. And the market applauded him, and rewarded him, and said fantastic, you are growing into Africa. So, everybody said, yes, great idea, you are going into Africa. Until the reality of the risk, which in fairness no one had anticipated, no one spoke about it. *The Economist* had this whole thing about Africa rising and it was, Africa was going to be the next emerging market, the new China,' De Ruyter explained. 'If it had been just me, or just Nampak, or just the Nampak board that had been stupid, I think you could say differently … but the entire market said, this is what you have to do. It still didn't go better after I left, things in Angola and Nigeria didn't recover. The debt was just unsustainable. With that level of debt, you really are … it's a millstone around your neck.'

De Ruyter said he gained excellent experience at Nampak, learning quickly over the four years he spent at its helm. He also had the full support of the board under Mboweni as chairperson.

'He said a couple of times, you need to go and run Eskom.'

While De Ruyter maintains that 'many in the investment community' understood that Nampak's fall was not of his making, the share-price collapse was among the leading criticisms that circulated when news broke of his appointment to Eskom in late 2019.

'In my first engagement with staff at Eskom, I took this head on and I said, you know, let's talk about Nampak, and I said this in front of an audience – the Franklin Auditorium was, in pre-Covid days, filled to the brim with overflow in another room – with all the executives, and I said, you know, here was a company, top of its class, really doing well but with too much debt ... any resemblance?'

The disastrous expansion of Nampak, De Ruyter said, also exposed a lot of historical complacency. But, he added, the adversity he experienced put him in a better position to tackle Eskom.

'I think if you had come from a highly successful industrial corporation where you never had any issues, and things went swimmingly and you had a very good system in place, everything would have worked well. I think Eskom would have been much tougher.'

He explained that Nampak had taught him the intricacies of the nature of massive debt and working capital.

'I venture to say that prior to my arrival at Eskom, working capital was something that was ignored. It just didn't matter. We had between R1.3 and R1.6 billion in spares per power station, being abused and stolen. We had a R1.3-billion write-off at Tutuka, when we couldn't find the spares.'

De Ruyter said he took the Eskom job out of a sense of national duty, a desire to contribute.

'But I was under no illusions that it was not going to be difficult,' he said.

In fact, he would realise just how difficult it was going to be within days of taking office.

8

The first battle

DAYS AFTER ARRIVING AT ESKOM, De Ruyter set in motion a series of events that would come to dominate his first two years in office.

It started on 10 January 2020, when he attended a meeting of the investment and finance committee (IFC), a subcommittee of the board that considers submissions on major financial decisions and makes recommendations to the overall board. He had noticed that the IFC was being asked to consider a budget increase for a five-year fuel oil tender – an increase of R4 billion, from R14 billion to R18 billion. It was one of the biggest expenditure items in Eskom's annual procurement spend, which is more than R140 billion.

In his time at Sasol, which has historically been Eskom's largest fuel oil supplier, De Ruyter knew that 'handsome profits' were made by selling the stuff, essentially a by-product of the oil-refining process, to the power utility.[1]

Fuel oil, or heavy fuel oil, is used as a primer when the boilers of generation units are started up – the fuel oil is burned before coal dust is introduced. The more start-ups a unit has, after a breakdown or coming back online after repairs or maintenance, the more fuel oil is used. Per litre or per ton, fuel oil is not expensive, but Eskom's fleet of 15 coal-fired power stations all use fuel oil – and lots of it. Between the 2013 and 2021 financial years, Eskom spent R24.8 billion on 3.5 billion litres of fuel oil, a significant share of which was paid to Econ Oil, a company owned and operated by Nothemba Mlonzi, an attorney and one-time acting judge.

Econ Oil – born of South Africa's noble procurement policies, introduced to provide recourse to those who were historically excluded from the economy, namely black economic empowerment – has its origins in a conference attended by Mlonzi around 2001. Among the presenters at the conference, held in Durban, was a senior Eskom official, Thandi Marah.[2]

Mlonzi had by this stage already registered Econ Oil and was looking around for opportunities. After the conference, she sought out the Eskom official, whose presentation apparently spoke to her interests. The official facilitated a meeting with Eskom's technical team, who explained to Mlonzi that in order for Econ to qualify to submit a bid, she would have to seek the backing of a 'South African oil major', have a technical person in her team who understood not only the product but also how Eskom did business, and obtain an ISO certification. They gave her the name of Johan Loots, who had worked for Sasol for 35 years, managing its fuel oil contract with Eskom. Sasol had been the power utility's sole supplier of fuel oil since 1987. According to Mlonzi, Eskom 'assisted' Econ Oil in concluding a deal to transport fuel oil on behalf of Sasol.[3]

As a result, Econ started earning money from Eskom in 2003, initially working out of offices located within Sasol. In 2012, Econ got its big break when it was awarded a major five-year fuel oil supply deal, which saw the company responsible for the majority of Eskom's 15 coal-fired power stations. The following year, Econ built its own blending plant in Marble Hall, Limpopo, to which then public enterprises minister Malusi Gigaba was invited. (It would later emerge that Marah forwarded a letter from Mlonzi requesting the minister's presence to the department's director general.)[4]

In mid-2016, with the 2012 contracts due to expire on 30 March the following year, Eskom started the tender process to place contracts for a further five-year period, from 2017 to 2022. A new tender was advertised in August 2016, but after eight months of technical evaluations of the more than 120 responses, Eskom discovered it had given potential suppliers the incorrect volumes for various power stations on which to quote prices. As a result of this error, the board tender committee scrapped the entire tender and Econ was kept on as a supplier to most of the utility's power stations on a month-to-month basis. On 17 May 2017, the board tender committee gave Eskom officials the green light to issue a closed tender to Econ Oil and the utility's other fuel oil supplier, Fuel Firing Systems (FFS) Refiners, for a one-year contract to allow time and space for a new long-term contract to be placed after another thorough tender process.[5]

But other suppliers came onboard during the closed tender process and, as a result, Econ lost five power stations to FFS – all told, Econ was allocated nine, while FFS increased its supply from two power stations to seven (one station was shared between them). Mlonzi met with Eskom days after the 12-month tender was awarded to complain that Econ had lost 68 per cent of the volume it had previously supplied and that officials were not taking into account the infrastructure in which Econ had invested over the years.

The new 12-month contract was set to expire on 30 June 2018, but Eskom once again failed to meet the deadline. The award of the tender would only be decided at the next board meeting on 16 October. For reasons that will become clear in the following chapter, the tender was ultimately cancelled, paving the way for Econ to be awarded further contracts to supply fuel oil to Eskom during 2019. It also bid and was ultimately awarded an R8-billion portion of the new five-year supply contract that was eventually concluded in October 2019.

Between 2003 and late 2018, Eskom paid Econ Oil more than R15 billion for fuel oil. Econ was not a manufacturer but effectively played the role of middleman – buying most of its fuel oil from Sasol and other local refineries (and apparently importing some from a company in Dubai) and onselling it to Eskom, with an undisclosed profit margin, according to court papers. Econ and Mlonzi strongly dispute this. Econ also supplied Eskom with diesel over the years, but the value of those contracts is unknown. What concerned De Ruyter, however, was not that Econ was up for an R8-billion share of the new five-year supply deal, but that the budget increase was simply not properly motivated and, more importantly, Eskom did not have the money to increase its expenditure by R4 billion.

Before meetings, the agenda and supporting documents are circulated to all attendees, and De Ruyter looked at the motivation for the budget increase and was immediately concerned. He noted down some questions about the submission, including around the information provided regarding pricing – he felt it was far too vague for the committee to consider properly.

During the meeting, De Ruyter voiced his concerns. But there was a problem – the chairperson of the IFC, former MTN CEO and close ally of President Cyril Ramaphosa, Sifiso Dabengwa. 'Mr Dabengwa, the chair of the IFC, was not prepared to accommodate much debate on the matter,' De Ruyter said in court papers filed almost exactly a year later.[6]

According to De Ruyter, he told the committee that there was no budget to accommodate the increase. 'But the response was, yes, but let's expand the value of the contract anyway.' He told me that Dabengwa, whom he had never met or interacted with meaningfully before that day, dismissed his concerns with 'almost disdain'.

'Typically, in a listed entity, the CEO is given airtime at a board subcommittee meeting. So I was quite taken aback, and I thought is this how it works? You know, is the CEO just supposed to be quiet? Because I said, hang on, I'm sure we can save money here. We were paying too much, I felt, my gut feel told me something was off. And Dabengwa was sort of just saying this is what we are gonna do.' The response to his queries, De Ruyter said, was along the lines of 'you will understand, in the fullness of time, that this is how we do it'.

'I remember walking out of that and thinking, this is different.'[7]

It was the first incident that would alert De Ruyter to the enormity of the mess he had walked into, he said. He described what followed in his affidavit filed in the High Court a year later: 'I thus formed the immediate impression that Eskom was not sufficiently concerned about keeping the costs of fuel oil down. I was fortified in this view when I considered the IFC documents, which were far too perfunctory, and did not offer a proper analysis of pricing.'[8]

THE FIRST BATTLE

The IFC did not approve the budget increase, but De Ruyter did not leave the matter there. He took immediate action to start investigating the tender and his first step was to ask Solly Tshitangano, the CPO and one of the three Eskom officials who had approved the memorandum to the IFC seeking the budget increase, a series of probing questions on 12 January 2020 over the tender process and award.

Tshitangano responded by asking De Ruyter to help him appoint experts to assist Eskom to evaluate and analyse the tenders and supplier information, which, he claimed, he had been unable to do for a year. It was extremely worrying; essentially, Tshitangano was conceding that the utility, which had just resolved to award a R14-billion, five-year tender to various suppliers, did not have the technical expertise onboard to properly evaluate the information that led to the awards.

On 13 January, the commercial team that had evaluated the bids responded in more detail to De Ruyter's questions.

'The answers largely confirmed my concerns that the tender had been conducted in an irregular manner,' he said in his affidavit. It had taken De Ruyter a matter of minutes to examine the IFC submission and to pick up that something about the entire tender was off, while other officials were content to keep driving the process to finality, even considering increasing the budget by R4 billion.

It was the start of a protracted and bitter battle, which would result in Eskom going to court to have the tender award set aside and Dabengwa resigning after accusing De Ruyter of misleading the board. Tshitangano would be axed for poor performance and his apparent determination to support Econ Oil. In turn, he would accuse De Ruyter of racism for his attempts to have the fuel oil tender award set aside.

The resulting investigations would all clear De Ruyter but would require an enormous amount of time, energy and money to finalise – time that could have been better spent focusing on his job.

Econ argued in court papers that De Ruyter was predisposed and prejudiced against them from the start because he had acted so quickly.

De Ruyter dealt with this conspiracy theory definitively during court proceedings.

'Ms Mlonzi appears to assume, in the first instance, that I arrived at Eskom with no knowledge or background of the organisation. She considers that I acted too quickly, largely because she assumes that I only began to think about how to improve Eskom on the day I arrived,' De Ruyter's High Court affidavit reads. 'But that is not so. I not only have valuable experience from the perspective of Eskom's suppliers (as a former senior employee of Sasol), but I also did extensive research before assuming my position at Eskom. I had engagements with Boston Consulting Group and McKinsey, both of which had done work for Eskom, and I also engaged with current and former suppliers. Therefore, by the time I arrived at Eskom, I had a reasonably good sense of certain priority focus areas. One of these focus areas was fuel oil. I knew from my time at Sasol that Eskom was the country's largest consumer of fuel oil, and that Sasol made handsome profits on the sale of fuel oil to Eskom. Therefore, together with other cost-management strategies, I flagged procurement of fuel oil as part of a broader strategy to contain costs.'

De Ruyter had set himself on a collision course with Dabengwa and Econ. He had just kicked a hornets' nest that would result in 18 months of vitriolic attacks that would test his resolve to remain at Eskom to breaking point – nearly resulting in his departure from the utility just months after taking the job.

Shortly after the IFC meeting, he sent his list of questions to the commercial team that had evaluated the fuel oil tender and then learned of a preliminary report that had been submitted to the utility the previous year by Bowmans, at the end of January 2019, concerning the improper conduct of former senior Eskom official Thandi Marah. Marah had worked closely with Econ Oil over the years and Bowmans had found evidence of a potentially improper relationship between Econ's Mlonzi and Marah – which included Marah's alleged unethical and inappropriate behaviour with regard to Econ, such as requesting 'sponsorships' from Econ Oil and failing to declare those that were in breach of Eskom policies, including a R100 000 donation to the ANC on 23 April 2014. At the time, Marah was deputy chairperson and treasurer for the ANC's Liliesleaf Farm branch.

According to a subsequent forensic report by Bowmans in October 2020, individuals involved in the process said that Marah had also contributed to delays in securing a new long-term deal. During negotiations for the awarding of the 12-month tender, she had emailed all the tendered and negotiated prices for each power station to Mlonzi, including those of Econ's competitor, FFS. When Mlonzi tried unsuccessfully to convince the Eskom official who managed the process to change the allocations for the 12-month contract, she called Marah to intervene. Marah in turn authored memoranda to various board committees seeking approval for the modification of the contract so that Econ and FFS could continue to supply fuel oil to Eskom.[9]

'Based on our findings we have found instances where Mlonzi was party to inappropriate and unethical behaviour, and in particular attempts to unduly influence Eskom offices, to inappropriately and unlawfully act to the benefit of Econ Oil, either during procurement processes and/or contract execution stages, this is amongst other things a serious breach of the Supplier Integrity Pact and may also amount to criminal conduct,' the Bowmans report read.[10]

Its findings, Bowmans said, gave rise to at least a reasonable suspicion that there existed a corrupt relationship between Mlonzi and/or Econ Oil and Marah. The report recommended that Eskom approach the police to open a case for further investigation while it took steps to reconsider Econ's position as a supplier for its breaches of Eskom policy. Marah told *Bloomberg* in April 2021 that she had no knowledge of the Bowmans report and, according to the publication, declined to comment further.[11] She was also approached by News24 with a set of specific questions relating to the findings in the Bowmans report. In response, she reiterated that she was not aware of the report and that Bowmans' investigators never spoke with her.

She asked News24 to send her the report, which was by then in the public domain, and emphasised that she and Eskom had reached an agreement that she be allowed to take early retirement on 31 January 2019.

Documents in the Eskom Files show that Marah was allowed to retire after she was served with a notice of suspension. Marah denied the charges Eskom was planning to bring against her, which were formulated based on the Bowmans report.

Mlonzi dealt with the findings of the Bowmans report of 14 December 2020 in detail in her answering affidavits in court proceedings. She expressly denied any wrongdoing and accused unnamed Eskom officials and De Ruyter of 'conjuring up' allegations against Econ to escape the contract it contended came into existence in late 2019 after Econ signed an acceptance letter following the tender process. The court disagreed that a contract was ever concluded, but Mlonzi was emphatic in her denials: 'The allegations levelled against Econ ... have no merit at all. Eskom knows this, which is why it has done nothing about them for over six years, in some instances.'[12]

Mlonzi also dismissed the Bowmans reports and McKinsey findings as containing allegations that have never been substantiated.

'The high water mark of Bowmans' allegations is what is said to be "inappropriate and unethical behaviour" and what Bowmans alleges is "reasonable suspicion raised in this report that there existed a corrupt relationship". To the extent that these are attributed to Econ, I deny them completely,' her affidavit read. 'I must mention that none of the issues investigated by Bowmans had anything to do with the 2019 tender. They are simply peddled by Eskom in order to paint Econ in a bad light. This is again in accordance with the stratagem adopted by Eskom to escape the contract concluded pursuant to the 2019 [sic], apparently in order to save costs.'

In one important section of the affidavit, Mlonzi addressed the findings by Bowmans directly: 'The first allegation is that Marah allegedly interfered in numerous procurement processes to the benefit of Econ, and the implication as I read the report is that either I or Econ requested that interference. I deny this.

'The report is also replete with allegations that Marah played a "major role" in Econ's development. That is an overly broad allegation which I deny to the extent with the history I have set out above. I do, however, admit that Marah offered assistance and guidance within the confines of her role. She was involved in transformation at Eskom, and she supported and assisted all women-owned, and black-owned companies involved with Eskom as far as she could within the confines of ethical prescripts. As a custodian of the transformation process at Eskom, she defended Econ where necessary, but she also pulled us back into line when called for, having even threatened us with contract termination at times.'

Mlonzi further held that Econ had invested significantly in its own infrastructure, at Eskom's insistence, so that it grew to a company that added considerable value to the supply chain and, furthermore, played an integral role in ensuring security of supply to Eskom for a strategic commodity that has a direct bearing on Eskom's ability to run its power stations and produce electricity.

She dismissed implications in the Bowmans report that she believed cast aspersions on the original tender awarded to Econ by Eskom in 2003.

'The next complaint registered is that, when Econ was awarded its first tender with Eskom in 2003, it added no value to Eskom. The award of the 2003 tender was a combination of both Sasol and Eskom fulfilling their transformation obligations by assisting the entry of Econ into the fuel oil market. That in turn assisted both Eskom and Sasol in achieving compliance with transformation policies. Over and above that, Sasol had discounted its usual prices for and to the benefit of both Econ and Eskom,' she stated.

'So called commercial value adds were not the only basis on which bids were evaluated at the time. Bids were also evaluated accordingly to hefty equity and supplier-development components. New market entrants, specifically those who were black and women-owned, scored highly on bids provided that they could guarantee continuity of supply at affordable rates. Econ fulfilled those requirements and was awarded the tender on that basis. In any event, the 2003 award has not been set aside. It stands as valid, and neither Eskom nor Bowmans has adduced a shred of evidence to show what the bidding criteria were at that stage, how Econ scored, or that Econ was awarded the bid unfairly.'[13]

Mlonzi admitted that she asked Marah to facilitate the presence of former public enterprises minister Malusi Gigaba at the opening of Econ's blending plant in Marble Hall in 2013, but maintained there was nothing improper about this.

'I admit that I told Marah that I would like for the Minister to attend the event, and that Marah was happy to facilitate it. There was nothing improper about that. As I have explained above, government had been aggressively pursuing a policy of transforming the energy sector. Econ's development (of which Marble Hall was a point of pride) was a transformation success story, and a positive manifestation of government's policies due to collaboration between state-owned entities (in this case Eskom) and private companies like Sasol. Marah had been involved in Eskom's transformation division. Her job was to support transformation. She had told me on numerous occasions that she was proud of Econ's growth, and of Eskom's involvement in helping to expand the fuel oil supply market which had ultimately enabled Econ's entry into that market, and their ultimate success.

'For these reasons, the Department, and Eskom were both desirous of using the opening of Econ's first blending plant as a platform to raise awareness of the success of government's transformation policies. Marah, and the Minister were enthusiastic about Econ's success story. That is why they were involved in the opening of Marble Hall. Enthusiasm of this sort is not an indication of corrupt relationships, and Bowmans tenuous assertion to the contrary is wrong and unfortunate. There were no corrupt relationships.'[14]

She denied that Econ had ever performed poorly in terms of its contracts with Eskom, except for a brief period in November 2017.

THE FIRST BATTLE

Just as Bowmans was about to embark on a fuller investigation into Eskom's dealings with Econ, in February 2019 the law firm's mandate was suspended by CPO Solly Tshitangano and legal head Jerome Mthembu. It would be terminated three months later.

Mthembu challenged News24's reporting about this, and was successful in a subsequent Press Ombud appeal. News24 was directed to apologise to Mthembu for stating as fact that he had halted Bowmans' mandate to hamper investigations into Econ Oil and former Eskom acting CEO Matshela Koko. The appeal panel, headed by retired judge Bernard Ngoepe, found that Mthembu had not been responsible for the Econ Oil investigation.[15]

Tshitangano cited this ruling in his responses to me as evidence that he was not responsible for managing the Econ Oil investigation when asked if he agreed he had breached his fiduciary duty to Eskom in not pursuing the matter after Bowmans' draft report of January 2019. Both Tshitangano and Mthembu strenuously deny that their actions against Bowmans were linked to Econ, but the report on Marah, which included damning information about Econ, was filed away and the investigation was left to stagnate for a year.

Around the same time, Econ, which had been suspended as a supplier in December 2018 pending the investigation, was brought back into the fold and was allowed to bid for the very five-year tender over which De Ruyter would grapple with Dabengwa. Mlonzi disputed in court proceedings that Econ was ever suspended. In March 2021, Eskom again suspended Econ as a supplier, a decision Econ is challenging.[16]

De Ruyter set about gathering more information. Within days, he found the January 2019 Bowmans report lurking in the legal department. Eskom had approached Bowmans in August 2018 to investigate allegations of improper conduct against Marah and Econ Oil. On the basis of Bowmans' preliminary report, handed to Eskom sometime in late January 2019, the utility instituted disciplinary proceedings against Marah, who was already on suspension at the law firm's recommendation. However, after issuing a denial to the charges, she was allowed to retire at the end of that month before any proceedings took place.

This was not the worst of it: De Ruyter discovered something potentially even more worrying – a 2016 presentation based on a report by global consultancy McKinsey, whose own contracts with Eskom through Gupta-linked Trillian had been an international embarrassment for the utility. As part of an analysis to determine possible cost-saving avenues, at Eskom's behest, McKinsey had taken a look at fuel oil expenditure and found that Econ Oil had potentially overcharged Eskom for one grade of fuel oil by R379 million in the four years between April 2012 and March 2016.

The Bowmans report revealed that after McKinsey provided Eskom with this estimation, an attempt was made by Ntuthuko Zulu, the senior fuel-sourcing specialist who was managing Econ's contract, to further investigate the alleged overcharging by asking Mlonzi to provide more data to verify Econ's invoices. In effect, Zulu was pushing for Econ to supply the invoices showing how much it had paid its own suppliers for the fuel oil it was providing to the utility. In 2012, Econ had quoted prices that were in some cases 10 per cent cheaper than its competitors, but over the years it had become the most expensive supplier by some margin.

Mlonzi did not take kindly to Zulu's attempts to get to the bottom of the matter. In a letter to Eskom on 8 March 2017, she set out her opposition to Zulu's actions as follows: 'Econ is experiencing an unprecedented change in its contractual and business relationship between itself and Eskom which is calculated to summarily destroy Econ Oil with no trace of its ever existence [sic].'[17]

'In recent meetings,' Mlonzi complained, 'Eskom requested Econ Oil to submit its invoice in price per source. This practice is not known in commercial terms, moreover where there is a selling price mechanism agreed to.' In effect, she was refusing to divulge what her company had paid for the fuel oil it then sold to Eskom.

'The rationale pointed out by Eskom for this practice is that, in the recent years/months our price (due to price escalation) is higher than that of [our] competition,' she continued. 'An interesting part to note is that when it was lower our competition was never required to do the same.' It is unclear what evidence Mlonzi had to prove this statement, but her letter bears further exploration, because she immediately determined that the request by Zulu was racially motivated: 'Needless to mention, the competition of Econ Oil is a white owned company, which enjoys far less cost price for the product from Sasol and Total for a far less volume than Econ is uplifting.'

Mlonzi has never presented any evidence publicly either that Econ was paying a cent more than her rivals or that this was racially motivated. Econ's main rival was not Sasol – from which Econ procured most of the fuel oil it onsold to Eskom – but FFS, which has been a majority black-owned company since 2008. Its majority owner is Mkhuseli Faku, an Eastern Cape businessman who has worked in the petroleum industry for more than 20 years. The company is also part-owned by the Bud Group.

In her letter, Mlonzi railed against instances where Eskom had ordered fuel oil deliveries from FFS, and accused the utility of attempting to 'frustrate' Econ and deliberately attempting to nullify their contract. Nevertheless, she offered a discount across the board and asked that Eskom 'does not exercise the right to order from alternative suppliers until Econ Oil indicates that this should be so'.

'The offer [of] a discount was my attempt at offering a practical solution to the problem which seemed irresoluble [*sic*] because Eskom wouldn't tell me how they calculated the alleged overcharging, and I couldn't get all the price calculation information from Sasol to satisfy Eskom's queries,' Mlonzi later explained in court papers. Her parting shot was the request that Zulu be removed from managing Econ's contract. Zulu was duly sent to Kendal Power Station. Mlonzi would later say in court papers that she asked for Zulu's removal because she had been informed that he had met with an FFS official at the Oyster Box hotel in Umhlanga, which Zulu categorically denied in a confirmatory affidavit filed as part of court proceedings.

De Ruyter learned all of this in the days after the first IFC meeting of 2020 – and it caused him no small amount of disquiet. On 23 January, he prepared a submission to the board in which he set out his immediate, short-term priorities, which included cutting out intermediaries in coal-supply deals and reviewing the fuel oil tender with a view to cancelling it altogether in light of a board resolution taken a year earlier, on 30 January 2019, to procure fuel oil directly from refineries. It was in fact at that meeting that the cancellation of the current tender was first raised. On 30 January 2020, his first full board meeting took place, during which the board endorsed his submission, according to minutes of the meeting attached to court papers.

With a mandate secured from the board, he set about further investigations of the tender, including the appointment of a specialist consultant, Werner Mouton, to look at the technical information in the bids. As De Ruyter had suspected, the probes revealed that there had been no proper financial evaluation of the bids, technical inspections had not been done and, most seriously, the team had negotiated with the suppliers in respect of every power station, instead of only on the power stations on which they had bid the lowest prices.

The mandate to negotiate with each supplier for every power station had been granted by the IFC, chaired by Dabengwa, ostensibly to rectify the inability of Eskom officials to undertake a proper financial evaluation of the bids. But, De Ruyter argued, in doing so the team had completely undermined the entire competitive nature of the bidding process, rendering the process irregular. Tellingly, Econ had originally bid lowest for eight power stations, but after negotiations was awarded further power stations, apparently on the basis of lower pricing.

In early March, De Ruyter requested that board chairperson Professor Malegapuru Makgoba circulate a round robin resolution for the cancellation of the five-year tender award – for reasons which included the apparent lack of expertise in the commercial team that had rendered them unable to properly evaluate the bids, that procurement from Econ Oil and

FFS went against a previous board resolution that Eskom seek to contract directly with major refineries, and that investigations had revealed possible collusion between the bidders – Econ had bid lower prices than Sasol, in circumstances where Econ procured most of the fuel oil it onsold to Eskom from Sasol, Total and Engen.

Makgoba duly circulated the round robin resolution, but it was instantly met with opposition. 'I have a major problem with this submission,' Dabengwa wrote on the same day to the Eskom board. 'I cannot support it and it goes to the heart of the procurement governance and process issues this company continues to be plagued with.'[18]

He set out a detailed list of points explaining why he was opposed to cancelling the award, including that the resolution motivating the cancellation did not contain evidence that Eskom had not secured the lowest prices. Furthermore, he said he was unaware that Thandi Marah, whom he did not name in his email, had left Eskom as a result of allegations of fraud and corruption, crucially revealing that the board had not seen Bowmans' January 2019 report on Marah. He also raised a concern that major refineries had been excluded from De Ruyter's 23 January submission, and said the allegation that there may have been collusion between bidders was unsubstantiated. Calling for evidence that the board had discussed the potential cancellation of the tender during the board meeting of 30 January 2019, as he did not recall such a discussion, Dabengwa said, 'I cannot accept' the assertion that the team did not have the requisite skills to properly evaluate the bids.

'Clearly management for whatever reason have been not in a hurry to conclude this tender, and this has been outstanding from 2017. In the absence of clear responses to the issues I have raised above, I will not consider this proposal and still expect management to implement the board decision as per the resolution,' Dabengwa concluded.

He was not alone in his opposition – Dr Pulane Molokwane, another board member, also objected. She felt that undoing a board resolution to award the tender via round robin was inappropriate and said, 'I'm really concerned about the continuous culture of delaying, canceling awards on some flimsy reasons.'[19] Similar to Dabengwa, she mentioned that Eskom's audit and forensics division had investigated and dismissed previous allegations of corruption.

Dabengwa's and Molokwane's reservations were not unfounded, albeit misplaced. In fact, a previous five-year tender process had been cancelled – to the benefit of Econ Oil – when allegations were made about corruption. It was during this investigation that audit and forensics picked up further information that was eventually investigated by Bowmans – resulting in the Marah report. It is curious that this report was never shared with the board.

De Ruyter responded with a further submission on 19 March 2020, setting out his key findings so far and tabling it for discussion at a board meeting on 25 March.

The minutes of that meeting show the matter was discussed extensively, with De Ruyter setting out the findings by Bowmans which had resulted in Marah's suspension and that she had subsequently retired before a disciplinary hearing could be convened, how Bowmans' mandate had been cancelled before a final report could be provided, and the deficiencies with the tender process.

But, it appears from the minutes, Dabengwa was not buying it.

'Mr Dabengwa raised concerns with regard to the extremely serious allegation against management for providing false information to the board in order to substantiate and motivate the cancellation of this tender. He stated that the information provided to the board had no relevance to the matter at hand, but it was provided as if it was specifically relevant to the tender that management was proposing to be cancelled,' the minutes recorded.[20]

There was further debate and, eventually, Makgoba called for a vote. Seven out of ten board members voted to cancel the tender – with Dabengwa, Molokwane and Professor Tshepo Mongalo dissenting. On the same day, Dabengwa emailed Makgoba, asking for his guidance on how to take the matter forward and confirming he was accusing De Ruyter and his team of deliberately misleading the board by presenting the allegations made against Econ Oil and the findings of the initial Bowmans report as being relevant to the current tender.

It is clear from his complaint that Dabengwa believed that De Ruyter, by presenting evidence to the board that Econ had acted improperly in the past, was trying to mislead the board into approving the cancellation.

In early April, Dabengwa said he wanted the matter investigated independently. Makgoba asked him to crystalise his complaint so that De Ruyter could respond, and thereafter the board would plot the course. On 29 April, Dabengwa sent his previous emails recording his dissent in the March board meeting, but did not finalise a single submission detailing his complaints expressly. Nevertheless, De Ruyter responded – and he came out swinging.

'Three members of the board strongly argued for the retention of the Econ contract,' he wrote in a 28 May 2020 submission. 'They have maintained their position ever since despite having had access to the substance of the information contained in this submission and the annexures thereto. The position of these board members is untenable.'[21]

Dabengwa had, in his own words, levelled 'an extremely serious allegation' against De Ruyter and his team. In his submission, De Ruyter wrote: 'The GCE [group chief executive, i.e. De Ruyter] concurs that this is a very serious issue. By necessary implication, an accusation of this gravity levelled against the GCE is an equally serious issue and goes to the heart of the relationship between the board and management. Making allegations of this nature against the GCE without the required adequate evidence is more than merely problematic, but fatally undermines the level of trust that is required for a constructive relationship with the board.'

De Ruyter had not been idle during the intervening months, and his submission showed this. Shortly after Dabengwa made the allegation, he had called Michael Katz, a well-known and respected lawyer.

'I had thought to myself, am I stupid? Am I missing something?' De Ruyter said of the incident. 'So, I phoned Michael, to soundboard this. And he said, no, absolutely, you are doing the right thing, which gave me a lot of confidence, because I mean he is sort of the doyen, the guru of corporate governance in South Africa. So that helped.'[22]

Katz had also provided a legal opinion on 11 May 2020. His fighting spirit sufficiently stoked, De Ruyter went on the attack. It was apparent, he wrote, that the board had not been provided with critical information, namely the McKinsey report and the Bowmans report among others.

'Mr Dabengwa's position on being apprised of this information appears to be that it was disclosed with the intent to mislead and deceive, and that the board would be better off labouring in a state of ignorance, wilfully disregarding highly pertinent information that clearly would have had a bearing on the board's award of the tender, had it been made aware of such information at the time of awarding the contract,' De Ruyter wrote. 'To aver that finding of previous, highly irregular behaviour by a bidder should be ignored when considering a new bid is an exceptionally captious contention. By this logic, Eskom should have no compunction in entering new business relationships with inter alia McKinsey, Tegeta, Deloitte, Tubular and others, because any irregularity occurred in the past and is therefore expunged from consideration if a new contract is entered into. This is clearly not the case.'[23]

As a parting shot, De Ruyter called for a board resolution not only exonerating him from wrongdoing, but also approving that a High Court application be launched to set aside the tender award and that Dabengwa be provided with a specified time to respond to De Ruyter's charge that his 'allegations were false, unfounded and unnecessary and thus calculated to bring the reputation of the GCE in disrepute, undermine his operational authority and inhibit him from taking the necessary steps to comply with his legal duties'.

De Ruyter later said that he was not sure if he had been expected to 'roll over and die'.[24] Confronted as he was with Dabengwa's serious allegations, he had pushed back. But the event, occurring so soon after he assumed office, nearly resulted in his departure from the power utility.

'To accuse the chief executive of misleading the board, as Dabengwa himself said, is incredibly serious. It's huge. It goes to the heart of the trust relationship between the executive and the board. And I phoned Makgoba, and I said, look, either he goes or I go, but I can't serve on a board where I'm not trusted,' De Ruyter told me.

Dabengwa, for his part, did not back down and responded in early June 2020, addressing further issues to which he sought a response – he maintained that De Ruyter had made unsubstantiated allegations of fraud and corruption and potentially collusive practices, and maintained his position that the board had never decided to procure fuel oil only from refineries and that De Ruyter had further failed to provide proof of this.

'Failure by the GCEO to specifically address the above requests will lead to the inference that his averments were made recklessly and without due regard to the proper administrative process,' Dabengwa wrote on 8 June. 'Furthermore, the conclusion [that] may then be arrived at is that there was a failure to discharge a proper duty of care.'[25]

Makgoba and the board had no choice but to initiate a full independent investigation and Advocate Wim Trengove, one of South Africa's foremost legal minds, was asked to oversee the probe. In a report issued to Eskom on 14 July 2020, Trengove absolved De Ruyter.

'Mr De Ruyter's statement that the board had adopted a new strategy on 30 January 2019, to procure heavy fuel oil only from refineries, was in all probability correct. Mr De Ruyter in any event made the statement honestly and had good reason to do so. Mr Dabengwa's accusation that Mr De Ruyter had made the statement dishonestly, was baseless and irresponsible,' Trengove wrote in his report.[26] On the other issues, he found De Ruyter had not misled the board either.

Dabengwa resigned a week later, on 21 July 2020, the same day the board adopted the Trengove report. According to a *TimesLIVE* report, in his resignation letter to public enterprises minister Pravin Gordhan, he said the Trengove report had not dealt with the core issues of his complaint. 'I believe it is not in the interest of Eskom for me to continue to serve on a board where there are such fundamental differences of principle with other members of the board,' Dabengwa wrote.[27]

The public would only learn of the drama months later when, in early October, the board released the Trengove report publicly, after it was leaked to the media.

9

'You're just bullshitting'

I spoke with Dabengwa in February 2022. The entire Econ Oil debacle was marked by a distinct lack of examination of the facts, he told me. He furthermore maintained that De Ruyter had purposefully misled the board.

'I haven't changed my position from what I have said,' he stated, reaffirming that he stood by his allegations and denying that he had been pushed to resign.[1]

As we have seen, Dabengwa took exception to the issues raised in De Ruyter's January 2020 submission to the board, specifically the allegations of corruption and fraud that implicated Econ and Eskom officials and that Econ had been allowed to bid in circumstances where the board had decided to procure fuel oil directly from refineries.[2] He asked for evidence of the alleged corruption and claimed that no such board resolution existed.

It becomes very complicated very quickly after that. It is perhaps necessary to take a closer look at the apparent leeway with which Econ had been allowed to operate. As set out in the previous chapter, Eskom and empowerment policies gave birth to Econ Oil, which first started earning money from the power utility in 2003. By 2018, Eskom had paid Econ more than R15 billion.

The long history between the two companies is punctuated by several key events, which De Ruyter detailed more fully in his submission to the Eskom board on 28 May 2020 in response to Dabengwa's allegations against him. In the early days, when Econ first started working with Eskom, it entered a 'logistics deal' with Sasol, which came about with the assistance of then Eskom employee Thandi Marah.

At that stage, Econ added no value to Eskom.

'It operated from offices inside Sasol's offices, all its deliveries were conducted through Sasol and presumably it was not possessed of any start-up capital either,' De Ruyter wrote in his submission.[3]

Over the next few years, it appears that Eskom officials rearranged things internally so that Econ Oil's account moved to a division directly under Marah's control. At the time, Econ supplied fuel oil to only two power stations. By 2012, it would be supplying 14 of Eskom's 15 power stations. It's competitor, FFS, supplied two (they shared one between them). When Econ lost five power stations to FFS in 2017 after the closed tender process, Econ's owner Mlonzi went on the warpath. 'This resulted in extensive interference by Mlonzi who met with Eskom officials, wrote letters and demanded that her allocation be increased,' De Ruyter noted in his submission.

With a new five-year tender to award, the board was set to decide at a meeting on 16 October 2018. But immediately prior to the meeting, a 'mysterious' whistleblower made allegations of corruption and fraud around the tender process, meaning the board could not discuss the tender award, as it now first had to investigate the claims.

While a probe by Eskom's internal auditors revealed the allegations were without merit, in the process they learned of Marah's apparent interference in favour of Econ over the years. The board subsequently cancelled the tender and recorded that the transactions were 'subject to investigation and confirmation that [an] alleged senior manager was not connected to the contract'. According to De Ruyter, this was a reference to the first Bowmans investigation, which at that stage was under way.

Marah's suspension followed, but then things became murkier still.

A submission prepared for the board on 23 January 2019 recorded what had been discussed at previous board meetings, what had transpired with the allegations made by the anonymous whistleblower, that Bowmans had undertaken a new investigation into fresh allegations against Marah, and that their report was due any day now.

The board met on 30 January, but the Bowmans report was not tabled, even though it had been submitted the previous day. Crucially, however, the minutes of the meeting record the following: 'The CPO [Solly Tshitangano] was mandated to take the necessary steps, provided that the business is not put at risk, to consider the pros and cons of the refineries option, which according to the CPO can be done in a short period of time on the basis that the current contracts/negotiations are cancelled based on the allegations which came to light.'[4]

'The minutes therefore clearly reflect an intention to source directly from the refineries but left the CPO with the authority to review the position depending on the veracity of the allegations against Marah and Econ Oil,' De Ruyter wrote in his own board submission more than a year later.

On 1 February 2019, Treasury wrote to Eskom in response to a letter received that same day from Tshitangano, which apparently requested Treasury's support for the implementation 'of the optimum procurement approach approved by the board' and noted that the board had directed Eskom management to procure fuel oil, diesel and liquid sulphur 'directly from the refineries/manufacturers'.[5]

It is necessary to highlight again that, in 2016, McKinsey found Econ had potentially overcharged Eskom by more than R300 million in a single financial year, 2015/16. It was now two years later, and as the investigations dragged on, Econ was still supplying fuel oil to Eskom based on a 2012 allocation from which it was able to profit significantly.

Despite this, and despite the board awaiting the outcome of the investigation into Marah and Econ, Eskom issued a further tender aimed at refineries in February 2019. It included Econ Oil, which ultimately won a large share of the three-month supply deal starting on 16 May. Eight days later, on 24 May 2019, Eskom issued a new five-year tender and allowed Econ to bid again.

'Yet the content of the McKinsey and Bowmans reports ought to have excluded Econ from both these bids,' De Ruyter wrote. 'The answer to these inexplicable events appears to lie in the fact that neither the Bowmans interim report [of January 2019], nor the McKinsey report, nor the internal investigation into Marah's conduct was ever disclosed to the board ... A final report from Bowmans was never obtained as their mandate was terminated during May 2019 just at the time that its contents would have been terminal for any Econ attempt at obtaining a further tender award.'

Tshitangano, it would transpire, was intimately involved in halting Bowmans' work, according to documents I have seen, which include an email from the SIU to Eskom in early 2019. These documents make it clear he was involved in meetings and part of the push to halt Bowmans' work. The firm would only be asked to complete its investigation exactly a year later, in May 2020.

Meanwhile, the new five-year tender was trucking along. Econ bid, as did FFS. But Engen, BP and Sasol also bid.

'It follows that Econ was now bidding against its own supplier in that whatever bid was awarded to Econ would in turn have been sourced from Sasol,' De Ruyter noted. 'The fact that Sasol appeared to have entered a bid in an amount higher than Econ does not definitively prove collusion, but it is an indication of at least serious irregularity. In the meantime, it has come to the CEO's notice that Sasol assisted Econ in compiling and executing its bid documentation. These are all events that require further investigation and effectively implicates both Sasol and Econ in unlawful conduct ... Econ as a reseller is simply not capable (without going insolvent) of discounting its price to Eskom at a level that is cheaper than would have been the case had Eskom simply purchased directly from Sasol.'

Despite all this, Econ was still allowed to bid and was supported at key junctures by various senior Eskom officials, which in my view includes Tshitangano, despite his denials.

There were problems around the evaluation of the May 2019 tender as well, mainly that no proper financial evaluation could be undertaken due to the differing pricing formulas used by the various bidders. But it got worse. Engen did not complete some of the bid documents; BP, which apparently quoted the lowest price for the most plentiful grade Eskom required, was disqualified because it could only ramp up volumes four months after the date of the award; and Sasol, which submitted a sterling bid, curiously could not meet all Eskom's requirements. All this meant that resellers such as Econ had to be included.

At the end of the day, as previously noted, in October 2019 Econ was awarded an R8-billion portion of the new five-year supply contract. To add to the controversy, it later emerged that Econ failed to disclose to Eskom that it had not yet secured back-to-back agreements with its own suppliers. Tshitangano, to his credit, stood firm on this when it came to light shortly after the tender award was communicated but before the contracts were concluded.

Faced with these facts, as well as the Bowmans and McKinsey reports, and De Ruyter's various submissions, Dabengwa still refused to back down. He maintains he was right to raise the matter.

'If you want me to be very specific, my allegations were, one, they put forward a statement that said that the board had made a particular resolution, which was investigated by Wim Trengove, and Wim Trengove never found any resolution of that nature,' Dabengwa told me.[6]

In fact, Trengove found that, faced with the minutes and the correspondence between Treasury and Tshitangano, De Ruyter was right to accept that the board had probably decided to procure from refineries. Dabengwa, however, says this is nonsense.

'There was never such a resolution, but they decided to say it's possible that the board made that decision. There is no self-respecting board that is told that it's possible you made the decision. It's either in the minutes, and it's reported, or it doesn't exist,' he insisted. 'Tshitangano is not a board member. You see this kind of nonsense that a manager can write to someone and say this is what the board said when he is not a board member, and that becomes the gospel truth, that is nonsense!'

Dabengwa claims that, to this day, no one has produced any evidence to back up De Ruyter's original January 2020 submission to the board that there were allegations of corruption and fraud involving Econ Oil. While it is true the board had not seen the reports at the time De Ruyter asked them to give him a mandate to cancel the tender award in court, they did appear in De Ruyter's submission in response to Dabengwa's allegations.

I asked Dabengwa what he thought after reading the reports.

'The Bowmans report we saw long after these meetings. And the Bowmans report, if you knew, Bowmans ... is saying that this report is now just what they were told by Eskom management. Bowmans is not standing by that report,' Dabengwa replied. He said he read that in a newspaper, but I was unable to find any such story, so I checked with a senior Bowmans source. 'He is talking shit,' this person told me.

In fact, as of March 2022, Eskom remained embroiled in protracted arbitration proceedings against Econ Oil wherein it was attempting to recover R1.2 billion for alleged overcharging between 2012 and 2018, based on Bowmans' reports. The utility also had reason to believe that other suppliers had been overpaid, and an investigation was ongoing.

'I am asking you where has this overcharging been proven?' Dabengwa demanded during our interview. 'And the point I am trying to make, at the time of submitting by the CEO and management the motivation seeking to cancel the contract, the issue of overcharging was never there.'

This is correct, but he surely became aware of it in March 2020, when De Ruyter responded to his initial allegations and repeatedly referenced the 2016 McKinsey report. Despite this submission, Dabengwa persisted in his request for an independent investigation, according to correspondence attached to court documents.

'I am talking about at the time the decisions were made. The reason I took this position I took; I am not interested in anything else ... For my purposes, I was totally unaware of Marah and things that Marah did. Totally unaware,' he told me.

What did Marah do? As touched on earlier, according to Bowmans she was very busy, but not with Eskom work. Marah had, they found, interfered extensively in the bidding process to favour Econ Oil, attempted (and failed) to add a specification to the tender that each bidder have its own blending plant (Econ had built one in 2013), disclosed confidential tender-pricing information to Econ by sending FFS's negotiated prices to a private email address used by Econ's Mlonzi, actively resisted attempts by Eskom officials to interrogate Econ's invoices, and insisted on being part of a WhatsApp group that was set up around Econ's day-to-day interactions with Eskom when she had no legitimate business reason for being on it. She had also received sponsorships from Mlonzi in her capacity as the ANC's Liliesleaf Farm branch treasurer – money that went to the party and other events.[7]

Mlonzi admitted to making the donation to the ANC, and further admitted to making a R10 000 payment to a 'Women in Dialogue' event at Marah's request. But she denied this was improper in court papers.

'I deny the existence of any gratuitous relationship, I however, admit making the payments and advancing the donations as alleged. I fundamentally believe in all the causes to which I donated and, more fundamentally, Bowmans does not allege that either Marah or I benefitted personally or that Econ benefitted at all,' Mlonzi said.[8]

It turned out Marah was a director of 33 companies, all registered between 2000 and 2016. Her husband and brother were directors of 12 and 8 companies respectively. In 12 years, Marah had failed to appropriately declare these interests. One of her companies and two of her brother's did business with Eskom. Furthermore, Bowmans found, she had done extensive private work during Eskom work hours without approval.

Dabengwa reasons that none of this should have formed part of the decision-making around the new five-year tender in 2019 because none of it related to that specific contract. It's worth repeating: Econ was awarded 14 power stations in 2012 because it had tendered significantly lower prices than its competitors, but it later grew to be the most expensive supplier. When Eskom, sitting with a McKinsey report that said Econ had overcharged by more than R300 million in a single year, tried to get information from the company about what it was paying its own suppliers, including Sasol, Mlonzi issued threats and called for the removal of Ntuthuko Zulu, the contract manager. Mlonzi would later explain in court proceedings that she held a reasonable apprehension of bias on Zulu's part, because he had placed orders with a competitor for a power station allocated contractually to Econ Oil.[9]

'And then you get this lawyer who was supposed to do, in my mind, an independent investigation, by the name of Wim Trengove, which like I said, was a whitewash,' Dabengwa told me.[10]

When I asked again if he maintained his position, he responded: 'Ja, of course, absolutely. Remember, we were dealing with a particular contract, not what has been happening over the last 10 years. There was no historical allegation put forward, and no evidence that was put forward. That's the point I am trying to make, that this issue that there was an overpayment, or there was overcharging, this came out a year later. But I can tell you that ... all of those people started getting employed, auditors and forensic people, and endlessly, I don't know how much Eskom has spent trying to find evidence, and how much legal fees have been spent. But life just carries on.'

I asked Dabengwa why he didn't sit down with De Ruyter to discuss the issue and try to reach a resolution if he felt so strongly that he was right.

'No, no, no, no,' he said. 'Let me explain to you. The reason is because I was chairman of the investment committee, so I had participated in all these processes. I knew the facts, I knew who presented what, I knew everything, and then when we had the board meeting, right? Clearly, for example, when I said, show me the minutes that show that this decision was made. And it wasn't shown, it wasn't shown then. And then I said, show us the evidence, I mean that's how boards work, when you go to a board to motivate something, there is always evidence for the cancellation or the arithmetic, or the facts to support what you are saying. But in this case, there was nothing.'

Dabengwa alleges that Trengove 'completely' ignored everything he said to him.

'I have been a director, I have been a CEO all my life, if I see a letter that says the board made this decision, and another board member questions it, the first thing I would do is I would go to the company secretary and say let me see the minutes. That's the first thing I would do. I would go to the company secretary and say let me see the minutes of that meeting. Boards make decisions every day, now if somebody who is not a board member can just write a letter, and by the way, normally when somebody does that, they would include a copy of the resolution, it's a standard practice,' Dabengwa told me.

I pointed out that it was not only Trengove who agreed that De Ruyter had acted correctly. Advocate Michael Katz had provided a legal opinion on 11 May 2020, also supporting his actions.

'To me that is all nonsense, whether it was Katz or it was whoever, if you don't put forward the resolution that the board made that decision, you're just bullshitting, all you are doing is you is [*sic*] trying to maintain a particular narrative, and that is why we are in so much shit as a country today,' Dabengwa lamented. 'People are not interested in facts. I mean, Katz himself, Michael Katz himself should have said whether there is a resolution of that nature or not, but what does he do? He writes a whole long story about how De Ruyter is acting in the interests of the company. Bullshit.

'You know, Trengove asked me that question, whether I thought it was a mistake or not, and I said no it was not a genuine mistake, because if it was a genuine mistake, when I corrected it at the board meeting, they would have said, oh, sorry, we made a mistake.

'It was never a genuine mistake. Because … this was discussed before I resigned, when this was presented at the board meeting and I said, uh-huh, show us the resolution, show us the minutes, so the fact that he is now aware that there are members of the board who do not agree with this, and if it was a genuine mistake you would go back and check and then come back and say, sorry, I cannot find these minutes, so that's why I will never believe that it was a genuine mistake.'

During the 45 minutes I spoke with Dabengwa, it seemed that no number of facts would dissuade him from his view that De Ruyter acted incorrectly. Yet those same facts, revealed in documents and investigations, show that Econ Oil not only enjoyed a remarkably close relationship with Eskom, but also, it seemed, evoked a fierce defence of its standing with the utility, for reasons that remain unexplained.

Despite Dabengwa's continued protestations, De Ruyter was vindicated and had seen off his first major attack, which had consumed an inordinate amount of energy and time.

But, as it always is at Eskom, trouble was brewing elsewhere – and Econ Oil would again feature as the golden thread.

10

The second battle

Days after the Trengove report absolved De Ruyter of wrongdoing in the Dabengwa debacle, he found himself sitting across a table from two detectives from the Sandton police station at Eskom's Megawatt Park head office.

He had been accused of a crime and the detectives were there apparently to undertake a thorough investigation just days after a complaint was laid by Econ Oil's managing director, Nothemba Mlonzi.[1] Their very presence stood in stark contrast to the failure of the South African Police Service to take any serious steps against dozens of former Eskom officials, including former CEOs, where tangible evidence of corruption involving multibillion-rand deals had existed for years.

De Ruyter was not accused of corruption or of allowing a family of politically connected businessmen to pillage Eskom's coffers. Rather, he stood accused of criminal defamation stemming from an Eskom press statement.

The statement, issued on 31 July 2020, was short and to the point. It confirmed that Eskom was taking legal steps to cancel a tender awarded to Econ Oil in 2019 for the supply of fuel oil. While the statement did not mention it, this followed on the board resolution adopting the Trengove report on 21 July. As we have seen, Econ had been awarded the lion's share, more than R8 billion, of a R14-billion tender in circumstances where it should never have been allowed to bid at all.

'A review of the circumstances leading to the tender being awarded to the company revealed serious irregularities in the process, including inflated prices charged to Eskom when lower priced alternatives were evident,' the statement read. 'Eskom has written to the supplier notifying them of its intention to have the contract terminated through the legal process.'[2]

For Mlonzi, the statement was apparently a declaration of war. Seemingly desperate to discredit De Ruyter, who was apparently determined to obtain cheaper fuel oil deals by cutting out the middlemen, of which Econ Oil was the main one (it blends limited grades of fuel oil and imports and buys the remainder), she returned fire by opening a case of criminal defamation against him. Weeks later, she would also institute a civil suit seeking R2.5 million in damages.

And so, with uncharacteristic alacrity, the two detectives set up a meeting with De Ruyter one August day. Their intention was to obtain a warning statement. Whether they actually intended on pursuing the obscure charge of criminal defamation remains unclear, but De Ruyter believes it was designed purely to intimidate him.

'So, I have my lawyers lined up, Aslam Moosajee is there from ENS and my personal advocate, Clive van der Spuy – who also comes from Bronkhorstspruit. Working at Eskom having your own lawyer is, I think, a prerequisite,' he told me with a hint of a smile. 'They [the cops] were quite junior, I think one was a detective constable. They tried to ask a number of questions. But between Van der Spuy and Moosajee they quickly batted them away. Then they said, okay, but we still need to take a warning statement from you, which they then duly did.'

After taking the warning statement, one of the detectives remained behind – to ask De Ruyter for a job at Eskom.

'Of course, I was afraid this was a trap, like I am trying to bribe him or whatever. So I said, no, send your CV to HR. I don't tell him, no, fuck off, are you bribing me or what, are you trying to entrap me? But it didn't surprise me too much,' De Ruyter recalled. 'I thought it was Kafkaesque. You know, here I am, and essentially, I am being told, just like Josef K., the main character in *The Trial*, just confess, just confess. But to what? No, you know you are guilty, just confess. It was, to my mind, a patently absurd set of circumstances. It was almost literally incredible.'

THE SECOND BATTLE

As of March 2022, both the criminal and civil defamation cases against De Ruyter were ongoing. The previous November, Independent Media's *Daily News*, a publication based in KwaZulu-Natal and a regular proponent of Econ's position, ran an article about the criminal complaint, revealing that Mlonzi's lawyers had written to the Sandton police station commander demanding answers as to why no arrest or prosecution had taken place.[3]

On 12 October 2020, a month or so after Mlonzi lodged the case against De Ruyter, Bowmans, which had been reappointed to finalise its historical work in May 2020, provided a forensic report on Econ Oil to Eskom. It was damning. Mlonzi, together with Marah, had interfered with the awarding of tenders; had asked for and obtained, through Marah, the confidential prices quoted by her main competitor FFS; and Econ had underperformed on its contract for years.

The following month, November, Bowmans provided a second report, estimating that Econ had, over a number of years, overcharged Eskom for fuel oil to the tune of roughly R1.2 billion. On the strength of this, Eskom reported a case of fraud and corruption to the Sandton police station, appending the report, and instituted arbitration proceedings to secure the return of the R1.2 billion it believed was unlawfully paid to Econ. Econ maintains its innocence and vehemently disputes that any overcharging took place.

In January 2021, Eskom launched High Court proceedings to set aside the five-year tender award from late 2019. It was ultimately successful. Econ filed for leave to appeal, which was denied in July 2021. A subsequent petition to the Supreme Court of Appeal filed in November 2021 was dismissed on 28 January 2022.

Mlonzi argued in her answering affidavit filed in opposition to Eskom's application that the utility 'has no honest belief that it does not have a valid contract with Econ. It also has no honest belief that any of the allegations levelled against Econ have merit. If it did, and in light of the seriousness of these allegations, Eskom would not have continued to procure services from Econ.'

So, why *did* Eskom continue to procure from Econ Oil, even after it had received the draft report on Marah, which included worrying information about Econ? Eskom had suspended procurement from Econ, only for this to be resumed later during 2019, after Bowmans was out of the picture – just in time to bid for the next five-year tender.

But Bowmans would later complete its investigation, and, on 11 November 2020, Eskom's supplier review committee chaired by chief procurement officer Solly Tshitangano was asked to review Econ's eligibility as an Eskom supplier. Tshitangano's apparent reluctance for the committee to discuss the matter set him on a collision course with De Ruyter. Tshitangano, it turned out, was another of Econ's fierce defenders.

Mmbulahiseni Solomon Tshitangano, known as Solly, was a respected figure in the South African public service for years prior to joining Eskom in January 2019. He had shot to national prominence in 2010 when he blew the whistle on controversial textbook tenders awarded to EduSolutions by the Limpopo department of basic education, where he worked in the finance division. He was subsequently dismissed. He fought his dismissal, eventually taking the matter to the Labour Court, where it was settled in 2013. That same year, he joined National Treasury with a well-earned reputation as a whistleblower and dedicated public servant.[4]

A key figure in Treasury, one of the last bastions of government that had stood against state capture by the Gupta family and their associates, he had worked in the office of the chief procurement officer, as chief director for governance, monitoring and compliance.

Public entities often require permission from Treasury to cancel and award contracts or deviate from established procurement practices. Treasury also has ultimate oversight over procurement and can request information and take departments or companies to task if it picks up procurement lapses. Any government entity that wishes to deviate from procurement regulations in any way must obtain permission to do so from Treasury officials.

During his time there, Tshitangano played a key role in regulatory oversight and was, by all accounts, a fierce proponent of procurement law. He was intimately involved in assessing applications and deviations, and was considered to be one of the country's leading experts on government procurement legislation compliance. His appointment as Eskom CPO, effectively in charge of the largest expenditure budget for any single government entity in the country, did not raise any eyebrows. In fact, it was seen as part of the shift towards strengthening senior management at the utility, which had exceptional challenges to deal with. A key focus area was procurement – the wound at the utility that would not stop bleeding.

Tshitangano's conduct in the two years he spent at Eskom, however, would surprise many and fly in the face of his track record as a corruption buster. At the end of December 2018, Econ Oil had been suspended as an Eskom supplier pending investigations. For reasons that remain unknown, when Tshitangano assumed office on 2 January 2019, he set on a course to resuscitate Econ as a major supplier of fuel oil to Eskom by supporting the award of R8 billion in tenders to the company that, by all accounts, should have been excluded from bidding for further contracts at least until investigations were finalised.

In February 2019, Tshitangano and Eskom head of legal Jerome Mthembu suspended and later terminated Bowmans' overall mandate – just as the firm was gaining steam with its probes and was cooperating extensively with the SIU and the Hawks.[5] They justified their actions by pleading poverty and questioning the costs of the Bowmans probe, which had already made significant headway into matters where considerable recoveries were possible and were indeed later realised – including the repayment of R1.5 billion by ABB, an international company hired to build control and instrumentation systems at Kusile Power Station.[6] Tshitangano, however, denies that he was ever involved in suspending the mandate.

'Your background information to the question is based on the allegations made by Eskom which were never substantiated during the disciplinary hearing,' Tshitangano told me. 'Eskom alleged that I was involved in suspending cooperation of Bowmans investigators with the SIU and later, suspending the law firm's mandate. No documentary evidence was submitted during the disciplinary hearing to support such an allegation. The acting head of legal told the disciplinary that Jabu Mabuza [the late former CEO] terminated Bowmans mandate and that I was not involved in suspending Bowmans mandate.'[7]

Tshitangano also pointed to the appeal decision against News24, in which Mthembu said he never worked with Tshitangano to suspend the mandate.

The evidence, however, does not support their version – or their reasoning. I have seen correspondence confirming that Tshitangano and Mthembu, who argue that the mandate was actually suspended by Oberholzer and Cassim in July 2019, issued instructions to Bowmans to stop work at the behest of the SIU and raised concerns over the invoices Bowmans had submitted.

In my view, if Tshitangano and Mthembu were truly intent on saving Eskom money, they could have focused on the so-called free-text procurement – the practice whereby goods do not have to be purchased from a list of suppliers who have been pre-approved as cost-effective. Instead, items can be purchased from any supplier and at any price. As a result, Eskom was paying significantly inflated prices for various goods. The reason behind such procurement is almost always corruption. When De Ruyter arrived at Eskom in 2020, he discovered that a staggering 75 per cent of Eskom's procurement was done on a free-text basis. Among the products he and his team found to be purchased at significantly inflated prices were single-ply toilet rolls worth around R4.99 bought for R26 each, black refuse bags worth R2.99 purchased for R51 each, and a wooden-handled mop worth R39 purchased for R200 000.[8]

The SIU pointed out to Eskom that hiring new forensic firms would set the investigation's progress back by at least six months – and Eskom would in any event have to pay the new firms.

This was apparently not a priority for Tshitangano. Instead, he chose to focus his ire on Bowmans, the one company working hard to help clean up instances of major corruption. When De Ruyter came in and clamped down on free-text procurement by changing the utility's procurement rules, Tshitangano accused him of unilaterally abrogating power to his office.

Tshitangano would later claim that Bowmans had been irregularly appointed, despite the fact that, as a Treasury official in June 2018, he had approved an R80-million, six-month expansion request from Eskom seeking permission to allow law firms from an expired panel of attorneys to finalise existing instructions. The approval included Bowmans, which was already undertaking investigations in cooperation with the SIU and the Hawks, as part of an agreement between Eskom and the various law enforcement bodies.[9]

A further oddity that casts doubt on the financial argument for suspending Bowmans' mandate is that probes undertaken by the SIU are always for the account of the customer. No matter the service provider appointed by the SIU, Eskom would have paid for their services. Furthermore, any new companies hired by Eskom would have to traverse significant ground already covered by Bowmans and would bill Eskom for their trouble. Mthembu had been part of the original decision to ask Bowmans to cooperate with the SIU – a decision arrived at to save time and significant sums of money.[10] Mthembu and Tshitangano both maintain their innocence, however.

A former government official with whom I discussed the debacle around the costs of the Bowmans investigation told me in no uncertain terms that, as a journalist, I should always be suspicious when people complain about the costs of a probe. He asked me the following: Imagine if a family member was murdered and the police launched an extensive investigation to catch their killer. Would you ever ask how much the investigation cost, even if it took decades? So why, within weeks of taking up the job at Eskom – a company that spends billions of rands every year – was Tshitangano so concerned by invoices from one of the best forensic teams in South Africa, which was undertaking work that the entire country, including the president, was interested in seeing completed? Work that Eskom would always have to pay for, even if the SIU appointed a different firm?

Within months of terminating Bowmans' mandate and derailing efforts to investigate serious corruption, Tshitangano began signing recommendations to the board to award further contracts to Econ. When I questioned him, he denied ever making a submission to the board for approval. 'Submissions to the board were recommended by the IFC after receiving recommendations from [Exco Tender Committee],' he said.

According to the evidence, this is accurate. But it is potentially misleading. The Exco Tender Committee does make recommendations to the IFC, which in turn makes recommendations to the board. But Tshitangano was not as removed from the process as he seems to suggest.

On 23 July 2019, he was among three officials who approved a submission to the committee seeking a mandate to negotiate, but not conclude, contracts for the supply of fuel oil with numerous suppliers who had responded to the tender.

On 25 July 2019, he supported a similar motivation addressed to the IFC.

On 1 August 2019, the IFC met and approved the request for a mandate, giving the Eskom commercial team the authority to negotiate with the suppliers, and thus empowering them to negotiate with Econ in respect of Hendrina Power Station only (as it is the only power station that uses grade 2 fuel oil) for R853 million over five years.

But because financial comparison of the bids was impossible, the team negotiated with all suppliers in respect of all power stations. Econ emerged as a significant beneficiary of this process.

On 29 August 2019, Tshitangano and other officials approved a memorandum to the IFC setting out the results of the negotiations and asking the IFC to approve a mandate to conclude contracts with the companies that had, after negotiation, landed on the lowest prices. Econ's share of the

R14.2-billion tender had increased from R853 million to R7.9 billion, from one power station to ten.

The reason for this was that BP had told Eskom it would be a few months before they could ensure security of supply to the power stations, and they had only tendered volumes sufficient for two power stations. There was no reason given for why Sasol, which had originally also tendered, was more expensive than Econ, considering that Econ would purchase a large amount of its fuel oil from Sasol before selling it on to Eskom.

On 29 October 2019, the Eskom board met. The recommendation made to the IFC was discussed and approved based on the negotiated outcomes, subject to the board being appraised, through Dabengwa as IFC chair, of the rates per ton for each supplier and each power station.

On 4 November 2019, Tshitangano sent Dabengwa a letter setting out the prices per ton and power station.

Tshitangano would go on to play a crucial role in nearly derailing Econ Oil at this stage. During a meeting on 14 November, it emerged that Econ Oil did not have back-to-back agreements in place with its own suppliers. With the contract due to commence on 18 November, Tshitangano wrote a letter to Mlonzi and Econ.

He recorded that Econ would be afforded a 'reasonable time to submit signed agreements which show quantities committed by other suppliers' and gave Econ until 21 November to submit the agreements.

In a letter dated 15 November, Mlonzi undertook to attempt to submit the agreements by 22 November.

On 22 November, Econ duly submitted an agreement with Engen and two letters from Sasol and Total.

On 23 November, Tshitangano said in a letter to Econ that, 'in the absence of signed agreements between Econ Oil and refineries, it is not possible for Eskom to sign a supply contract with Econ Oil'.

He implied that Econ had misrepresented its ability to meet the contractual obligations and said Eskom would commence the process to reallocate Econ's portions of the tender to other suppliers.

Mlonzi hit back on the same day, saying that the acceptance letter she had signed on 8 November confirmed the existence of the contract, and furthermore that there had been no pre-condition in the letter of award for the back-to-back agreements to be in place: 'Econ Oil's argument that the letter ... did not have pre-conditions is unbelievable because a draft NEC 3-supply contract has not been finalised as yet and in that further pre-conditions were discussed at the meeting held on 14 November 2019.'

Tshitangano hit back harder, pointing out that Econ should have been aware of the requirements of a government entity in terms of contractual agreements, that it had submitted the Engen agreement late, and that letters from Total and Sasol did not suffice.

'Eskom will only sign a contract with Econ Oil based on volumes confirmed by back to back agreements and not commitment letters. Commitment letters were acceptable at bidding stage and not contractual stage,' he wrote on 26 November 2019.

He gave Econ until 6 p.m. that night to make any representations.

Mlonzi responded on the same day, providing the agreement between Econ and Total, and a draft agreement with Sasol, and disputing that Econ had received Tshitangano's letter of 14 November indicating the deadline to provide the agreements by 21 November.

On 27 November, Tshitangano pointed out that Econ had submitted a document from Sasol dated 2018. The following day, he provided further details of the date, time and to which email address the 14 November letter had been sent.

Despite this, on 29 November, Mlonzi wrote to another Eskom official requesting the start date of the contract, confirmation of the content of the contract and operational information.

On 10 December 2019, Tshitangano again approved a submission to the Exco Tender Committee asking for approval to increase the contract value by R4 billion, which was necessary because the original approved volumes at R14 billion had been submitted due to budget constraints. The actual projected volumes, the submission showed, would be significantly higher – from 1.8 million tonnes a year to 2.2 million tonnes.

The revised projections shuffled some power stations around, resulting in a drop in the total contract value proposed for Sasol from R6.5 billion to R6.3 billion, despite it getting two additional power stations.

Econ's contract value would have increased to R8.5 billion from R7.9 billion, while FFS would have seen an increased contract value of R3.4 billion from R1.8 billion, thanks to the addition of Kusile, which was originally allocated to Econ.

Again, a similar motivation was approved by Tshitangano on 7 January 2020, this time to the IFC. Oberholzer also approved the submission, but with a note – feedback on the process to date must be provided to the IFC.

It was this submission, discussed at the IFC, that caused De Ruyter's discomfort.

Tshitangano was not alone in approving these submissions, but as CPO he had a direct responsibility to prevent Econ from siphoning more money out of the utility. He tried to argue in a subsequent disciplinary hearing that Eskom had to continue trading with Econ until a court of law set the contract aside. This defence was rightfully dismissed. In light of his correspondence with Econ, it is also still unclear how the company was allowed to remain part of the tender process.

He told me that the court, and Cassim in his disciplinary hearing, had found that the board had erred in approving the tender award. '[The Exco Tender Committee] chaired by Calib Cassim, the chief financial officer, recommended the appointment of Econ Oil and others. The IFC chaired by Sifiso Dabengwa recommended the appointment of Econ Oil and others. The chief procurement officer was never a member of the [Exco Tender Committee] of IFC,' Tshitangano said.[11]

The conflict between De Ruyter and Tshitangano began in early February 2020, when De Ruyter invited his CPO for a discussion with HR head Elsie Pule over his apparent failure to achieve key objectives. Less than two months into the job, the new CEO had taken stock and recognised that Tshitangano was not performing well and suggested he move to a compliance role, where his expertise lay.

Tshitangano, apparently incensed, set in motion a strategy to cast doubt over De Ruyter's integrity. Eight days after the meeting, he sent a letter to board chairperson Makgoba, copying in the Presidency and Gordhan's office, accusing De Ruyter of victimisation, of irregularly appointing specialist consultant Werner Mouton in contravention of Eskom procurement regulations, and of targeting him for 'refusing to suspend procurement rules'.[12]

In response to my questions, Tshitangano denied that he performed poorly and further denied that the letters, which were publicly disseminated, were designed to discredit De Ruyter. 'I deny that I underperformed in my role as CPO at Eskom. Eskom made allegations which were never substantiated during the disciplinary hearing,' he told me. In fact, he said, Advocate Nazeer Cassim's report 'does not contain any finding on poor performance'.[13]

Subsequent investigations by News24 have revealed that Tshitangano's actions were not unprecedented. In 2005, years before he took up the position at the Limpopo education department, he was suspended from his job as chief director in the Mpumalanga provincial treasury on 11 charges of misconduct, charges that bore remarkable similarity to those he would later face at Eskom – failure to submit key documents on time, abusive or insolent behaviour towards his boss, and failing to report irregularities as soon as he became aware of them. When his performance was questioned, he filed complaints with higher political offices in the province, as well as oversight bodies. Most notably, he raised certain allegations of irregularities with the then MEC for finance, Elsie Coleman, on the same day he received a letter querying an alleged irregular salary increase for which he had self-motivated. The allegations to Coleman related to events that had occurred months earlier, begging the question as to why he had not reported them sooner.[14] News24 approached him for his views, but he did not respond. It is apparent, however, that the issues were not taken further, suggesting that any allegations of wrongdoing against Tshitangano were never substantiated.

Makgoba advised Tshitangano to file a formal grievance, but he did not do so. Instead, it was a year before Tshitangano took any further steps – when it became clear he was to be suspended following continuing allegations of poor performance. He had been tasked with saving Eskom 4 per cent of its annual spend of R140 billion on goods and services, but he had failed to do so. His disagreements with De Ruyter over procurement had reached an impasse, and he had failed to attend meetings with the CEO and other Eskom executives.

On 4 January 2021, in a letter sent to Gordhan, the Presidency and SCOPA, Tshitangano accused De Ruyter of racism; of abusing his power for changing procurement practices; of violating HR practices by hiring people for several senior positions, including company secretary and head of IT; and of targeting black-owned firms. White-owned companies were getting far better treatment, he alleged. He defended awarding Econ Oil more than R8 billion in further contracts long after Eskom became aware of a potentially improper relationship between Econ and Marah by saying that the utility could not lawfully preclude the company from bidding 'based on allegations'.[15]

By accusing De Ruyter of racism, Tshitangano abused the worst fears of South Africans, who for too long have struggled to lift the yolk of historical oppression and racial inequality. An allegation of racism against a white man in charge of a government-owned entity will never disappear, no matter how many people speak out in his defence or how many investigations clear him. It was an allegation designed to destroy De Ruyter and to cast those who supported him under the same cloud.

11

The allegations of racism

Towards the end of February 2021, Eskom finally suspended Solly Tshitangano for poor performance and for issues around Econ Oil and instituted disciplinary proceedings. Among the charges were his failure to timeously handle the internal processes to review Econ's position as a supplier, his role in awarding further contracts to Econ despite his knowledge of the alleged impropriety around the company's interactions with senior Eskom officials, and his breaching of confidentiality policies.[1]

A week later, Parliament's public finance watchdog, SCOPA, pounced on the allegations made by Tshitangano, particularly the inference that black-owned supplier Econ Oil was being treated differently from white-owned companies. On 3 March, SCOPA came out swinging, publicly announcing that it would launch a probe into the allegations of racism against De Ruyter. Tshitangano had laid the groundwork for this latest assault on the Eskom CEO by copying SCOPA in on his letters to Gordhan and the Presidency, which also ensured they were made sufficiently public.

On 15 March, SCOPA asked De Ruyter to respond to Tshitangano's allegations. In what appears to be a characteristic response, he hit back hard in a signed affidavit submitted to the committee at the end of March.

'The accusations and subsequent energy spent on dealing with them have seriously undermined my ability to properly and efficiently conduct my duties,' he wrote. 'In effect, a simple and straightforward operational issue dealing with underperformance has been elevated to Parliamentary level. This kind of spurious and defamatory accusation does not justify the enormous time and resources wasted in dealing with it. It seriously undermines morale in Eskom, as we seek to engender a high-performance culture. It obstructs the efforts made by all concerned to recover Eskom's productive efficiency. In addition, it constitutes a very serious imposition on me personally which distracts very significantly from my primary task of turning Eskom around.'[2]

Eskom decided to establish its own inquiry. On 9 March, it announced its intention to appoint an independent senior counsel to conduct a comprehensive investigation into Tshitangano's allegations. Advocate Ishmael Semenya was duly appointed on 1 April. A week later, at Gordhan's urging, SCOPA announced its decision to halt its inquiry to allow Eskom time to complete its own probe.[3]

In the meantime, Tshitangano's internal disciplinary hearing took place. On 28 May, panel chair Advocate Nazeer Cassim recommended the CPO's immediate dismissal, having found that he had acted intentionally to further the interests of Econ Oil. 'Matters which should have been dealt with internally were externalised for an ulterior purpose,' Cassim remarked, in a reference to Tshitangano's letters to Gordhan, the president and SCOPA. He also determined that the accusations of racism levelled against De Ruyter were a clear attempt 'to divert attention' away from Tshitangano's 'own wrongdoing'. The issue, Cassim found, 'had nothing to do with race'.[4]

In his trademark style, Cassim eviscerated Tshitangano's conduct: 'He made serious disparaging allegations based upon racial content and thereby injured the dignity of De Ruyter ... he did not testify before me to deal with this. It is clear the relationship between him and De Ruyter is irretrievably destroyed and the trust relationship between him and Eskom is irretrievably destroyed ... Tshitangano acted dishonourably and has exhibited all the qualities that makes [sic] him unsuitable for the position he occupies. He declined the opportunity to deal frankly with serious allegations of misconduct and which impacts on the employment relationship.'

Cassim was also scathing of the Eskom board and SCOPA, and found that Tshitangano had placed Econ's interests above Eskom's.

'The CPO was also given an audience by SCOPA,' he noted. 'Whether this was orally or by way of written representation is unclear to me, but again the theme is to discredit De Ruyter on racial grounds and the typical South African excuse when a person in the capacity of the CPO is confronted with wrongdoing, namely to play the race card. Race has nothing to do with this matter. This matter is about dishonesty and corruption. It is about competence and the kind of society we wish to live in and future generations to succeed or fail. It is a sad reflection of this country that we are so fragile that we cannot rid ourselves of subjective inadequacies in dealing with issues of efficiency and performance. The issue in this matter is the interests of Eskom and to permit the CPO to use racial overtones to undermine a proper investigation into the contracts awarded to Econ Oil and his own conduct demonstrates weakness on the part of the board of Eskom.'

On receiving Cassim's findings, Eskom served Tshitangano with a letter of dismissal.

'Cassim's finding was not based on facts placed before him in the disciplinary, but his opinion,' Tshitangano told me in a written response.[5]

The following week, on 1 June, Semenya handed over *his* report, in which he stated that Tshitangano had to be threatened with misconduct charges before he agreed to appear for an interview, only to then, in a singularly bizarre twist, deny that he had ever accused De Ruyter of racism.

'Where in the letter do I say André is a racist?' an excerpt from the interview transcript reads, quoting Tshitangano.[6]

'I must state in the most emphatic of terms that this retraction by [Tshitangano] is startling,' Semenya noted in his report. 'As a senior executive member of Eskom, he is alive to the fact that these complaints had enjoyed wide publicity, he wrote to the president of the Republic of South Africa, the minister of Public Enterprises, the director general of the department of public enterprises, the Auditor General, SCOPA, the Zondo Commission and to the National Treasury. Any simple Google search for "purging black suppliers" reveals names of [De Ruyter] referencing him as a racist. It also records complaints by organisations such as the Black Management Forum, calling for the suspension of [De Ruyter]. As a senior executive at Eskom, the CPO must have known the nature of these allegations, given the history of South Africa, would impair the dignity of the GCE, malign the entire board of Eskom and imperil the corporate standing of Eskom, which is the biggest state-owned company. The allegations could potentially harm Eskom's financial status.'

Tshitangano, Semenya said, never publicly denied the allegations despite knowing they were 'wrong, egregious, false, baseless and lacking any substantiation ... It is not surprising that the GCE would take umbrage at these scurrilous allegations; that the Chairperson of the board would take offence that he is cast as somebody presiding over a corporate entity that is accused of practising racial discrimination which, according to the CPO is promoting a "culture where corruption, nepotism and patronage are tolerated".'

On the question of racism, and given South Africa's history, Semenya described testimony by Eskom chairperson Professor Makgoba as follows: 'His evidence was that many of us may struggle to define what a lion is, but we will all know if it entered the room we occupy.'

In response to a question about why he never publicly corrected the narrative around his allegation against De Ruyter, Tshitangano told me he had reiterated to Semenya that De Ruyter was 'not consistent when treating suppliers'. 'My letters gave examples which show that De Ruyter was inconsistent in applying the rule of law. Semenya's report is based on evidence that was presented to him during the hearing. You must get the transcribed record in order to understand what transpired during the hearing.'[7]

He said Semenya ignored his evidence in two respects: Tshitangano believed section 195 of the Constitution was applicable to Eskom, but Semenya disagreed and recorded his dissent in his report. Tshitangano also said that he told Semenya the board never ratified the appointment of Werner Mouton, the fuel expert De Ruyter had brought in to evaluate the fuel oil tender, but that Semenya recorded in his report that Tshitangano conceded that the issue was moot because the board *had* ratified the appointment.

'It is not clear why you are not challenging Semenya's omission and factual inaccuracies,' Tshitangano said to me. 'Semenya refused to deal with the cancellation of the Econ Oil contract and other issues I have raised during the hearing which were not included in the terms of reference ... It is not a belief but a fact that De Ruyter applied the rule of law inconsistently. De Ruyter stated publicly that ABB will not be suspended from the supplier database.'

This is correct. But the reason, which Tshitangano apparently refused to accept, was because ABB's systems are an integral part of Eskom's power stations. They cannot be ripped out and replaced without massive cost and lengthy shutdowns. The company is also fully cooperating with investigations.

In support of his allegation that De Ruyter was treating a black-owned supplier differently, Tshitangano had pointed in his letters to Gordhan to an instance when De Ruyter questioned him over why he had not made himself available for a November 2020 meeting of the supplier review committee, which was due to discuss Econ's continued status as an Eskom supplier. Tshitangano argued this was a breach of governance, as the CEO was undermining him. He also complained that De Ruyter's instruction to limit transactions of R10 million or more, or with a life of longer than six months to require divisional board approvals, was further violation of policy and governance.

But De Ruyter was simply protecting Eskom amid a looming restructuring of the company – he had been tipped off that there was a sudden flurry of long-term contract placements, purportedly designed to survive the restructure.

'On whether the GCE's instruction of 31 August 2020 constitutes a breach of Eskom's delegation of authority of July 2020 or that it is an unlawful suspension of the board's power, the answer is, no,' wrote

Semenya. 'It would be perplexing that a GCE, whose compact with the Board and responsibility is to manage the day-to-day operations of the business can be unable to give such an instruction. It is surprising that the CPO, as a senior executive at Eskom, would find it necessary to raise this instruction as unlawful and address the president of the country. He should know better.'

In conclusion, Semenya wrote: 'Having heard all the evidence, and considered all the documents, I could find no substantiation for the allegation that the GCE has conducted himself in any manner that would amount to racist practice.' He similarly found no evidence of De Ruyter's or Eskom's alleged poor governance, or that any recruitment processes were irregular, or procurement practices unlawful.

De Ruyter's response to SCOPA, coupled with the Cassim and Semenya reports, must have been enough to satisfy the parliamentary committee, because it apparently never raised the spectre of its own investigation again.

'In Nampak I had this saying, if you are white and you are useless, I will fire you. If you are black and you are useless, I will fire you. So, the common denominator is, don't be useless,' De Ruyter told me in 2022.[8] He said this attitude resonated particularly with young black professionals, who all rose to the challenge.

'I think that one of the negative consequences of affirmative action has been that we have tiptoed around this issue of performance. And it does a disservice to ambitious, competent, professional, intelligent hard-working black people, who want to be rewarded for who they are and what they do,' he noted. 'I have to say in Eskom, we had a board meeting, a distribution board meeting. And again, fuck it, particularly young black women. Fuck it, they are good. They are smart, they are clever, they are competent, you ask them a stinker of a question, and they [snaps fingers] have the answer. And I ask, have you thought of this? Ja, we have and we have done x, y and z. And I sit there, and I think thank goodness. And that gives me a lot of confidence.'

THE ALLEGATIONS OF RACISM

By all appearances, Tshitangano had been part of a devious plot to rid Eskom of De Ruyter, and by extension Jan Oberholzer, while protecting politically exposed suppliers. He claims that he is innocent and had acted out of genuine concern. He also maintains that he is a whistleblower, and that it was as a result of his delay in executing the Econ Oil contract that De Ruyter acted against Econ Oil – paving the way for the High Court to set aside the award. Econ was subsequently denied leave to appeal by the Supreme Court of Appeal. It remains only for the arbitration proceedings – and criminal investigations – to be finalised.

What Tshitangano apparently had not counted on was his adversaries' resolve to fight for what was right in the face of his allegations against them. It cost him his job.

12

Smelling a rat

THERE IS AN ANOMALY IN Eskom's performance over the past decade that may hold valuable clues as to why the utility's power stations are currently experiencing a period of unreliability that is, in the historical context, and even taking into account their age, extreme.

During 2021, while De Ruyter fended off allegations of racism and incompetence, I undertook a challenging but important investigation into this anomaly in an attempt to try to come up with an answer as to why South Africans are so often left in the dark, an answer that the public would be able to understand. It took me and my colleagues at News24 down a rabbit hole into the minutiae of Eskom's technical performance data so often cloaked in the jargon of opaque key performance indicators.

Context is important, so let's start with this: power generation units are highly technical pieces of machinery that are precisely designed around water and coal quality, ambient conditions, and a range of other specifications. To overly simplify it, the units burn coal in massive boilers to generate heat, which turns demineralised water into steam, which in turn flows through a series of turbines that spin faster than the speed of sound at their outer edges – it is this motion that generates electricity.

One boiler and turbine are regarded as a single machine made up of different parts, like a car. This is a unit. Most of Eskom's power stations have six units. Each unit has variable performance characteristics over its lifespan – at the very beginning, there is an infant mortality period, where the unit is unreliable and difficult to manage until it has been fettled and poked and prodded until it runs well. It then enters a long period of functionality, provided the appropriate quality and quantity of maintenance is undertaken, before it experiences another stage of increasing unreliability as it nears the end of its useful life. Plotted on a graph over time, this will result in what is known as a bathtub curve, two peaks at either end and a long, deep trough in between.[1]

Medupi and Kusile are still, for the most part, in the infant mortality stage, which in power station terms could last years. And Kusile is yet to be finished. But the other 13 coal-fired power stations are all at the point where they are seeing an increase in breakdowns due to their age – in 2022, the average age of these power stations was 44 years. (According to one study, the average global lifespan of a coal-fired power station is 46 years, but many can continue to operate for 50 to 60 years or longer.[2]) I call these Eskom's 'legacy' coal stations to differentiate them from the newer units at Medupi and Kusile. Many of them are due for retirement in the next five to ten years. The problem is that these coal-fired stations make up around 90 per cent of Eskom's generation capacity.

Eskom loves to use the car analogy because everyone gets it – but a new car is not usually unreliable when purchased, because mass production ensures any major gremlins have been resolved before the car leaves the factory, with exceptions here and there resulting in recalls. Power generation units are not mass-produced – they are built to order by a range of experienced companies that each specialise in a specific part of the power plant. They also cannot be recalled to the factory – they are simply too big. For example, the structures that house the boilers at Medupi are 142 metres tall.

Just like cars, however, power stations require maintenance. Massive amounts of maintenance. These highly tuned machines demand to be treated with the care befitting an enormously expensive and nationally important piece of infrastructure. Eskom has struggled in this regard due to a range of factors, including that the utility has never had enough money to undertake all but the necessary maintenance and, because the country has been short on generation capacity for more than a decade, the units could not be taken offline – they had to run.

Government policy has played a huge role here. Since the late 1990s, with the roll-out of the massive electrification programme to connect more homes to the grid, Eskom had been warning that the country urgently needed to build more power stations. These warnings were ignored until 2004, when South Africa was announced as the winning bidder to host the 2010 FIFA World Cup. It occasioned the introduction of a 'keep the lights on' policy that effectively translated into power stations being run extremely hard. In 2008, load shedding was introduced for the first time.

Eskom had started building new power stations in 2005 and 2006 – notably the open cycle gas turbines Gourikwa and Ankerlig, and Medupi, Kusile and Ingula. They were all supposed to be completed by 2015 and 2016, but that did not happen. In February 2015, five years after the World Cup, Eskom recognised that the mantra of 'keep the lights on' was unsustainable. It had impacted on the utility's ability to do maintenance.[3]

For over a decade, power stations had been run to meet demand without any increase in maintenance to offset the damage. Instead of doing more maintenance and bringing major midlife refurbishments forwards, Eskom delayed due to money issues and system constraints. It was a toxic cycle that was next to impossible to break without shutting down entire power stations for a year or more for major refurbishments.

That is, until December 2016, when Matshela Koko was appointed acting CEO and, by all appearances, performed a miracle, ending the terrible cycle without any massive loss in electricity production. Koko, or Moses as he sometimes refers to himself, seemingly parted the Eskom Sea and turned the power stations around by simply being smarter and better than everyone else.

These claims, I thought, warranted a closer look. And as I grappled with the data and spoke to experts, I began to smell a rat.

Let's go back to April 2001, when the last unit of Eskom's 13 legacy coal-fired power stations came online at Majuba.

A key indicator that power stations use to measure performance is the energy availability factor (EAF). EAF indicates how much time a unit is available to produce electricity for the grid, but, importantly, does not necessarily indicate whether the unit is actually producing electricity.

EAF is calculated as follows: a unit rated 500 MW is capable, theoretically, of producing 4 380 000 megawatt hours (MWh) in a 365-day year. It undergoes a lengthy planned maintenance, also measured in MWh and expressed as planned capability loss factor (PCLF) – because Eskom has 'lost' the capability of producing electricity because the unit is offline. Some planned outages last 60 days or more. Called a general overhaul, the unit is serviced from top to bottom, at enormous cost.

Over a 60-day outage, our theoretical 500 MW unit will then 'lose' 720 000 MWh to planned maintenance. Our unit is a good performer, so we will assume that, in this year, it experienced very little unplanned capability loss factor (UCLF), which is also measured in MWh and simply refers to unplanned breakdowns. Over the course of the year, our theoretical unit breaks down unexpectedly on three occasions, losing a total of 25 days or 300 000 MWh.

In summer, the unit must run at below optimal capacity, because high temperatures result in the cooling systems struggling to keep the units cold. Over the three hottest months, the unit therefore loses 21 000 MWh due to being run at lower capacity. This is known as other capability loss factor (OCLF), effectively a catch-all measure for all losses that cannot in the normal course be attributed to unplanned breakdowns.

PCLF, UCLF and OCLF are all measured monthly as well as annually and are expressed in annual reports as a percentage of the overall theoretical capacity.[4]

So, in terms of our theoretical unit, the 720 000 MWh of planned maintenance, or PCLF, is presented at the end of the year as 16.4 per cent, UCLF as 6.8 per cent and OCLF as 0.4 per cent. EAF is then calculated by taking the full theoretical capacity, which would be 100 per cent, and deducting the losses:

$$100 - 16.4 - 6.8 - 0.4 = 76.4$$

Our unit has an EAF of 76.4 per cent for the year, which is considered good but not great. The problem with relying on this metric alone is that EAF simply shows the unit was *available* to produce electricity for 76.4 per cent of the time, but no unit runs at 100 per cent capacity even when it *is* available.

At night, for example, the load put on the unit is reduced. During the morning and evening peaks, it is ramped up to meet demand. This is all centrally controlled by the system operator, who sits in Germiston in a vast control room that shows how much electricity the more than 80 units Eskom has are producing.

There is another factor called partial load losses, which is usually included in UCLF figures. This is when a unit is run at below optimal levels, often because of a fault that requires the unit to be run at lower load, either because the fault results in the unit being unable to run at higher load, or because running the unit at full load with the fault could result in the unit breaking down. The most common causes of partial load losses are boiler tube leaks (the tubes located inside the boiler through which the steam is pumped), vacuum losses (basically a loss of pressure inside the unit) and coal mill breakdowns.

Each unit has a series of mills that grind the coal to a fine dust before it is blown into the boilers. Sometimes, more than one mill breaks at a time, meaning the power station cannot feed coal into the boiler at the required rate. As a result, the load on the unit is reduced so that the remaining mills can keep up. Coal mills break down due to normal wear and tear, but are designed to mill certain grades of coal, so when a different type of coal, or a load containing rocks, is introduced into the mills, whether by accident or on purpose, they break faster than expected.

Based on our example, if our unit is available for 76.4 per cent of the time, it could theoretically produce 3 339 000 MWh. But because it is never run at full capacity even when it is not being fixed or maintained and due to partial load losses, it produces only 1 736 280 MWh.

To measure how hard the unit is actually working, Eskom uses a key performance indicator called generation load factor (GLF). In our example, the GLF resulting from the unit producing 1 736 280 MWh is 65 per cent. The most important – and best – indicator used, however, is energy utilisation factor (EUF). EUF is similar to GLF but with a crucial difference – it calculates how 'hard' the unit was running when it *was* available – in other words, when the unit was actually running or standing by ready to be ramped up.

To calculate EUF, GLF is divided by EAF and expressed as a percentage. The EUF for our theoretical unit is, therefore, 85 per cent.

According to a senior Eskom official, an EUF of 80 per cent and above for coal-fired power stations is considered 'not ideal'. If your car's engine can rev up to 7 000 rpm, an 80 per cent GLF is like revving the engine up to 5 000 rpm – and keeping it there.[5] A nuclear power station such as Koeberg, however, should have an EUF of close to 100 per cent. Pumped storage stations and open cycle gas turbines operate only when needed, during peak, so they usually have a high EAF with a lower EUF.

Tracking these performance indicators over time can show us how well the power stations are performing, how much maintenance is being done, how often they are breaking down and, most crucially, how hard they are being run. It took me months – and hours spent with Eskom experts – to understand this, but once I did, I began examining Eskom's raw performance figures over the past decade in detail. I focused on the legacy coal-fired stations, the backbone of the utility's fleet, because, besides being older, they cause the most disruption when not available.

In June 2001, two months after Majuba's last unit was commissioned, the monthly EAF was 93 per cent, which is regarded as very good. Over the next decade, it declined every year without fail to 83 per cent in January 2012. Over the next three years, it dropped a staggering 13 per cent, to around 70 per cent by late 2015. This is to be expected to a degree, because more maintenance results in a lower EAF. But in the context of Eskom, the lower EAF was the result of a dramatic increase in unplanned breakdowns, which constrained the utility's ability to deliver electricity and, in turn, limited maintenance opportunities. It is therefore surprising that Eskom still uses EAF as an overall performance indicator. In driving a higher EAF, you are sacrificing maintenance.

But then Matshela Koko was appointed acting CEO of Eskom and something miraculous happened. EAF increased to 77.3 per cent in 2016/17, crept up to 78 per cent in 2017/18, then dropped back dramatically to 69.95 per cent in 2018/19.[6] Koko resigned in February 2018. The data shows that unplanned breakdowns at Eskom started increasing in the months before his departure and spiked sharply immediately after his resignation.[7]

EUF for the legacy stations showed a similar anomaly. In 2015/16, EUF was 92.6 per cent. During Koko's tenure as CEO, it dropped to 85.07 per cent in 2016/17 and remained relatively stable at 84.17 per cent in 2017/18. After his departure, it rose sharply again to 90.07 per cent in 2018/19. In 2019/20, it rose even higher, to 93.08 per cent, before dropping again to 90 per cent in 2020/21.

While this trend was to be expected, given the higher EAF, I felt a closer look was warranted, because the decreasing EUF belied what I was told actually happened on the ground. So, I dug deeper.

The overall picture presented in Eskom's annual statements includes figures from all the different types of power stations owned and operated by the utility. According to these figures, Eskom's overall EUF has remained between 70 and 80 per cent for the past few years. In other words, the true EUF of the coal-fired stations was being masked by the calculation of overall EUF.

Had Koko done anything over those two years that had resulted in this inexplicable and dramatic turnaround in performance? He could not have done less maintenance, because the figures for planned maintenance had increased too and Koko has widely claimed that he did more maintenance than anyone else. There were obviously fewer breakdowns, because UCLF figures had also dropped. And an examination of the data showed that the fortunes of the legacy power stations mirrored the overall picture, so it could not have been due to the addition of new units at Medupi and Ingula.

None of it made sense. Koko has repeatedly bragged that during his tenure, at the same time as EAF increased, he spent *less* on diesel to run Eskom's expensive open cycle gas turbines – in fact, spending on diesel dropped from R8.6 billion in 2015/16 to around R340 million in the following financial year. But the cherry on the cake was the fact that there was no load shedding from August 2015 to June 2018.

So, no load shedding, no running of expensive yet necessary open cycle gas turbines, a dramatic increase in overall reliability and availability, and a significant drop in unplanned breakdowns. To cap it all, GLF and EUF decreased, indicating that the units weren't being run as hard. This was all seemingly achieved overnight, as if by magic.

Eskom's new leadership apparently also thought something was off. Oberholzer asked Eskom's then head of audit, Ishan Bhowani, to look at the anomaly – the increase in EAF in 2016/17 and 2017/18 and its sudden drop in 2018/19. Bhowani delivered a nine-page memorandum to Oberholzer in late 2019.

The key periods he examined were the 2015/16, 2016/17, 2017/18 and 2018/19 financial years. In 2015/16, EAF was 71 per cent. It increased to 77.3 per cent in 2016/17, stayed at 78 per cent in 2017/18 and dropped to 69 per cent in 2018/19.

Bhowani found that planned maintenance decreased negligibly from 12.99 per cent in 2015/16 to 12.14 per cent in 2016/17. There was a similar negligible decrease from 10.35 per cent in 2017/18 to 10.18 per cent in 2018/19. But there was a major shift in unplanned breakdowns. Unplanned losses decreased from 14.91 per cent in 2015/16 to 9.9 per cent in 2016/17, but then spiked from 10.18 per cent in 2017/18 to 18.31 per cent in 2018/19. It was these unplanned maintenance figures that played the biggest role in the rise and fall of EAF over the same period, Bhowani concluded.[8]

It was not possible to determine the causes of the decrease and subsequent increase from simply studying the data, but Bhowani set out some 'possible scenarios' to explain the phenomena. First, he said, it was possible that units, instead of undergoing maintenance, had been run with partial load losses for extended periods, thereby 'deferring' full load losses. 'In the long run when the unit shuts down due to the partial load losses, the damage is more severe and down time for repairs is longer,' he noted. 'When the unit trips due to a fault, the power station may keep the outage period short (not fixing the problem properly) so the unit can come back earlier, preventing prolonged unavailability.'[9]

He used Kriel Power Station in Mpumalanga as an example. In 2017, Kriel reported the highest partial load losses. 'Units 1, 2, 4, and 6 ran with partial load losses for a period of between a year and three years,' Bhowani noted. 'During this period, planned outages were taken to fix certain issues but the problems persisted even after the planned outages. It is only when a general overhaul was scheduled and conducted that the problems were fixed.' Worse still, unit 5 at Kriel ran with partial load losses for an extended period until the main turbine eventually stopped working.

Another possible scenario, Bhowani found, was that power stations did not declare partial load losses until the system operator requested full load on the unit. Not declaring partial load losses, like not doing unscheduled maintenance, can artificially inflate EAF. According to Bhowani, in certain instances, the non-reporting of partial load losses could be 'inferred' from the system operator's request for full load. 'Based on the sample reviewed, it is reasonable to infer that the EAF could have been artificially inflated,' he found. 'It is probable that in reporting of EAF, not all partial load losses were reported/taken into consideration.'

When I put this to Koko, he called the suggestion 'preposterous'.

Bhowani also cited other possible factors that may have played a role, such as the 'inclusion of EAF in the performance incentive scheme' and a practice of penalising power station managers for outages, in possibly driving behaviour in the direction of maintaining a high EAF. This caught my eye.

Bhowani was obviously referring to a disciplinary 'card' system introduced by Koko in February 2016, in his capacity as group executive for generation, that saw power station managers either being paid handsome bonuses for meeting performance targets or facing periods of suspension without pay for failing to meet targets, which may well have incentivised widespread underreporting of faults and running units extensively – in some cases for more than a year, Bhowani found – with serious faults that required them to be later taken offline for lengthy periods for repairs.

In my own investigations, there seemed to be a clear correlation between the introduction of Koko's card system and a significant and sudden decrease in reported unplanned breakdowns at power stations in its immediate aftermath, followed by an increase in unplanned breakdowns almost exactly a year later, starting in April 2017, which spiked sharply after his departure in February 2018. Can I say, without any doubt, that the card system was solely responsible for the spikes? No. But we have to begin looking for answers somewhere and there's an important point worth bearing in mind here.

Performance data at Eskom is manually recorded by human beings. There is no automated computer system that captures this information. The officials at every power station report the performance of their units to Eskom's head office.

That's what made Bhowani's memorandum a bombshell. His findings suggested to me that Eskom officials could have potentially manipulated performance statistics because of a system that effectively incentivised them to hide breakdowns and punished them for reporting breakdowns.

I received Bhowani's document as part of the Eskom Files that were leaked to the Global Initiative against Transnational Organized Crime and shared with News24 in February 2021. At the time, I told my editor, Pieter du Toit, and my colleagues at News24 that it wasn't conclusive enough to publish anything just yet, but that it offered valuable clues. They humoured me and I set about gathering data. Lots of data.

In a subsequent Press Ombud appeal hearing, Koko accused me of obtaining and being in possession of the data unlawfully. But what the former CEO did not understand was that Eskom under De Ruyter was a much more transparent institution. I simply asked them for the data and access to officials who could help me understand it better. This stood in stark contrast to the South African government's general lack of transparency.

I must also mention that the same officials who assisted me, whom I cannot name, disagreed with my interpretations of the data in private and officially in responses to questions I posed to Eskom, often pointing out that the figures had been subjected to verification and audit.

The issues I grappled with in reporting on and analysing the data are complex and relate to thousands of moving parts at units across the country. It is impossible for anyone to constantly watch, take note of or prevent errors in not only the operation of the units but also the data that is captured by Eskom officials. In reality, there may not be one single explanation that answers these questions. But it is important that we start trying to answer them, as the data shows that after this period of apparent good performance, the power stations were far more unreliable.

And therein, I believe, lies another important detail. Eskom's auditor, SNG Grant Thornton, has not provided a reasonable assurance for unplanned maintenance figures included in the utility's annual reports since 2017/18 nor explained why. I asked them to speak to me about their processes and methods in providing an audit opinion on the key performance data in Eskom's annual reports at the time.

I never heard back from them.

In short, I felt that South Africans were being left in the dark about why they were being left in the dark. So, armed with Bhowani's memorandum and the data received from Eskom, I tried to determine how unplanned breakdowns had been so quickly and dramatically reduced during the period that coincided with Koko's tenure as acting CEO.

In response to detailed questions, Eskom called Bhowani's memorandum 'inconclusive' and said that no definitive answer had been found to explain the improved performance in the 2016/17 and 2017/18 financial years, but that officials believed an increase in maintenance in 2015 – a so-called 'maintenance festival' took place in December 2015 – as well as the introduction of new capacity from Medupi, Kusile, Ingula and IPPs all contributed to a system that was less constrained.[10] Eskom seemed prepared to leave it there.

The utility's reliance on the 2015 maintenance is worth noting. Let's look at the facts. At the time, Eskom had more than 80 generation units between its 15 coal-fired power stations. Yet 12 million MWh of maintenance, which contributed to a 3 per cent increase in planned maintenance in 2015/16 (to roughly 13 per cent overall), was undertaken on just *five* units at five power stations that were offline for between 140 and 300 days. Yet this planned maintenance is hailed as a key reason for the apparent overall turnaround in generation performance in 2016/17 and 2017/18. Furthermore, even those power stations that did not benefit substantially from the 2015 'maintenance festival' recorded an inexplicable decrease in unplanned breakdowns from March 2016. To me, this appeared to give further credence to Bhowani's theory that partial load losses may have gone underreported. This on top of an apparent real decrease in partial load losses.

Koko's tenure as CEO also coincided with a 4 030 per cent increase in the MWh equivalent of generation units that were placed in 'available cold reserve' (when a unit is not run because it is not needed) at the legacy coal stations between the 2015/16 and 2017/18 financial years – from 136 244 MWh in 2015/16 to 5.56 million MWh in 2016/17 and a further 10.3 million MWh in 2017/18 – officially because there was no load shedding and the system was less constrained.

'I remember that during 2017 on some days we would have something like 17 units on cold reserve,' one senior Eskom official told me.[11]

Koko left Eskom in February 2018. Notably, by the end of the 2018/19 financial year, there were only 652 000 MWh in cold reserve. The dramatic increase in units placed in cold reserve only to be brought back online almost immediately after Koko's departure raises serious questions.

Eskom rules state that if a unit is placed in cold reserve, the power station must be able to bring the unit back online within a stipulated time frame (referred to as call-up time) in case it's needed. Cold reserve is thus not a parking lot for broken equipment. In 2016/17, 5.6 million MWh of the legacy coal station units were placed in cold reserve, and in 2016/17 and 2017/18, a combined 5.8 million MWh of 'opportunity maintenance' was undertaken on various units in cold reserve. Opportunity maintenance can loosely be described as maintenance done when the opportunity arises – for example, one part of the unit causes it to trip and be taken offline, and another part of the unit is maintained at the same time. The correlation between the MWh in cold reserve and the MWh of opportunity maintenance undertaken during this period suggests that units may have been placed in cold reserve when there was a breakdown and repairs classified as opportunity maintenance to avoid reporting them as unplanned breakdowns and decreasing the key performance metric of EAF. Eskom disagrees. They said that, for the most part, the utility's internal quality control systems would have picked this up and the data would have been corrected.

Of more concern, however, is that in 2017/18, when 10.3 million MWh were placed in cold reserve, the equivalent in opportunity maintenance was not done, theoretically meaning that those units could be brought back online at a moment's notice. When, shortly after Koko's departure, most of the units *were* brought back online, this coincided with a marked increase in unplanned breakdowns. In my view, and given the absence of significant opportunity maintenance carried out at the time, this may suggest that the units placed in cold reserve were not all in perfect working order, as they should have been. In a number of instances, the data shows that units were taken offline for planned maintenance and then immediately placed in cold reserve after the outage ended, perhaps indicating that they were not repaired in the planned maintenance time frame and went into cold reserve where repairs could be done surreptitiously.

There is another element to this that reinforces my belief. In 2017/18, 7.3 million MWh of the 10.3 million MWh placed in cold reserve was recorded at five power stations: Kriel (2.1 million MWh), Komati (1.7 million MWh), Grootvlei (1.3 million MWh), Hendrina (1.2 million MWh) and Tutuka (1 million MWh). In the same year, unplanned losses for these power stations were at 18.85 per cent, 15.01 per cent, 26.29 per cent, 19.53 per cent and 14.38 per cent respectively.

The following year, 2018/19, unplanned losses rose dramatically at each of these stations: 33.45 per cent at Kriel, 22.98 per cent at Komati, 31.02 per cent at Grootvlei, 37.33 per cent at Hendrina and 26.53 per cent at Tutuka. The same five power stations recorded just 194 947 MWh combined available cold reserve that year.

From what I discovered in my investigations, Koko's disciplinary card system, linked to the performance of the power stations' units, appeared to be a key factor in this magical formula. According to his system, power station managers and other staff faced suspension without pay after receiving yellow cards. Nine yellow cards resulted in a red card. A red card was usually accompanied by a seven-day suspension without pay. Three red cards resulted in dismissal. Green cards, for meeting performance targets, could be used as credits to negate yellow cards and secure handsome performance bonuses.[12]

Koko was appointed group executive for technology in 2014, group chief executive for generation and technology in early 2016, and acting group chief executive in December 2016. Although he was suspended twice during his stint as acting CEO, the card system remained in place.

According to him, all maintenance and outage planning fell under his direct control from 2014 onwards. He denied that official performance figures were skewed by underreporting of unplanned breakdowns and stood by his controversial disciplinary system. 'There is no factual basis to allege that "the EAF was artificially manipulated",' he said in reply to a question posed by News24 in 2021.[13]

'People were scared shitless of him,' one senior Eskom official told me and my News24 colleague Azarrah Karrim. 'But you can't rule by fear forever.'[14]

This person related how Koko would equally praise good performance and come down hard on poor performance during open forums and said the card system perpetuated a culture of fear. As a result, Eskom lost many power station managers with decades of experience during Koko's tenure.

Koko called the allegations of EAF manipulation 'preposterous' and laid the blame for the utility's current problems squarely on the new management team. 'Fact is that the Eskom leadership is failing today and News24 must stop looking for scapegoats to cover up De Ruyter's dismal performance,' he said.[15]

But a former Eskom engineer told us how a power station where he had worked was run despite faults that would normally require either a partial or a full load loss because the station manager had two red cards and would be fired if a third was issued. Protection systems were also allegedly tricked into preventing an automatic shutdown. 'I remember we spent hundreds of thousands of rands a month on portable compressors, so that compressed air could be blown onto temperature sensors on the [coal] mill bearings,' this engineer told us.[16]

This would 'trick' the temperature sensors into not reading the high temperature levels on the mill bearings, which ground the coal into dust, thereby preventing the protection systems from kicking in, leading to severe damage to the equipment. On at least one occasion, this person said, danger tape was put up and a security guard posted near a unit to warn people off because there was a hydrogen leak in the generator. On another occasion, a steam leak in a unit also required a security guard to be posted to keep people away. At one point, a unit at Medupi exploded due to an error made by technicians trying to find the source of a hydrogen leak. It would cost Eskom billions of rands to repair.

I checked the engineer's version with Eskom by asking the utility to provide me with the monthly expenditure for portable air compressors. The power station said it needed the compressors because the station's built-in compressors, which had been running since the 1980s, were no longer fully operational. Between April 2016 and March 2018, Eskom spent R10.5 million hiring air compressors for the power station.

Koko, meanwhile, continued to deny that his card system incentivised power station managers to run units past breaking point and that officials hid partial load losses.

'This is very disrespectful to the power station managers that I know, and that I have worked with,' he said of the allegations. 'The power station managers I have worked with are very competent persons and they are loyal to Eskom. They would never do anything stupid. They are not suicidal. They are not thieves either.

'The engineering definition of running "units long after a stoppage was needed" is called an operating excursion. An operating excursion means a generating unit was operated outside of its operating and technical specifications.

'The power station managers I worked with would refuse to operate generate [sic] units outside of their operating and technical specifications. This is against the PFMA [Public Finance Management Act]. They are guardians of these generating units. They have the duty of care.'[17]

Koko also denied he was responsible for placing the units in cold reserve, saying such outages were approved by a dedicated committee within Eskom called the STERF committee, which received requests for outages of 14 days or more and had discretion to approve, deny or postpone such requests, depending on system requirements.

Eskom, meanwhile, explained that the increase in cold reserve hours was a direct result of the system being less constrained and therefore requiring less capacity. There is some merit in this, because the amount of electricity produced by Eskom overall was relatively similar over the years in question – there was no dramatic increase in demand; in fact, there was a slight decrease year on year. But, to my mind, this still does not explain what happened after Koko's departure.

I went back to what was happening on the ground. Bhowani had provided a basic analysis of partial load losses at Kriel Power Station over the EAF increase and decrease period. I decided to begin there.

Kriel Power Station, situated in Mpumalanga between the towns of Kriel and Ogies, was commissioned in the late 1970s. It has a nominal capacity of 2 850 MW and comprises six units that, in 2017, were rated at 475 MW each. Sometime prior to September 2015, a fault developed in the induced draught fan of Kriel's unit 5, which resulted in the unit being run with a partial load loss until March 2018, when the turbine on the unit seized. While the two are not necessarily related, between September 2015 and March 2018, an accumulative 25 days of short-term planned maintenance was carried out on the unit, but the fault in the fan was never fixed. It was only after the unit was taken offline for a 100-day general overhaul to repair the turbine that the induced draught fan was also repaired.

Meanwhile, on 24 February 2016, unit 1 registered 'vacuum high' on the main turbine condenser. It was run for nearly five months with this problem before the first unplanned breakdown occurred, which resulted in the unit being taken offline for just 39 hours. When it came back online, the problem persisted. Twenty days later, the unit was offline for six hours for a second unplanned breakdown. Again, the problem persisted. Another 20 days later, the unit was taken offline for planned maintenance that lasted 84 hours. The problem persisted. This was followed, a month later, by another 70 hours of planned maintenance. Again, the problem persisted. Twelve days later, the unit was offline for 38 hours, scheduled as 'unplanned losses'. Hours after coming back online, it was taken offline again for just under two hours. The problem still wasn't fixed. Over the next two months, an accumulative 148 hours of planned maintenance was undertaken, and during this time the problem was not fixed. Eventually, in January 2017, the unit was taken offline for 100 days for a general overhaul and the problem was finally solved.

The situation was virtually replicated in units 2, 4 and 6 during this period.

If it was true that the system was not constrained, as posited by Eskom and Koko, then it would surely not have been necessary to run these units for so long with these faults. Yet they were, and the short outages that were booked suggest that officials may have been avoiding getting yellow and red cards at any cost.

Furthermore, Kriel recorded the highest level of cold reserve in 2017/18, contributing 2.1 million MWh to the 10.3 million MWh placed in cold reserve that year. According to the data provided by Eskom, Kriel did not have a great year. It had an EAF of 62.75 per cent with planned maintenance at a respectable 18.29 per cent but unplanned losses at 18.85 per cent. It suffered 42 trips and generated just 13.2 million MWh out of a possible 24.9 million MWh, for a GLF of 48.8 per cent. EUF came in at 77.78 per cent, which, according to Eskom, was acceptable.

At first glance, these figures appear 'fine'. But they are not.

August 2017 saw the most units being placed in cold reserve at Kriel – a combined 520 212 MWh, almost a quarter (24.53 per cent to be exact) of the station's capacity for that month. Theoretically, the station was capable of producing a little over 2.1 million MWh in August 2017, which had 31 days, but Kriel also recorded 531 057 MWh of planned maintenance, 162 482 MWh of unplanned maintenance and 16 089 MWh of other losses. Adding what was placed in cold reserve, that made for combined losses of just over 1.2 million MWh.

So, in reality, Kriel was only ever going to be able to produce 890 559.11 MWh in August 2017. It generated 838 868.7 MWh – 94.19 per cent of what the units that were online were physically capable of producing.

There is another problem. Eskom records its planned maintenance, unplanned losses and other factors based on the total installed capacity of all the units – this is why GLF and EUF figures for Kriel are so low for August 2017 and why, on paper, it appears that the remaining units were not run hard. The reality is murkier. More detailed data on planned maintenance at Eskom's power stations showed a combined planned maintenance figure for Kriel in August 2017 of 438 325.01 MWh – the result of three short outages on units 3, 4 and 5, as well as unit 6, which was offline for the entire month due to an outage that started in June 2017 and ended in October 2017. (The difference between this total and the official recorded total of 531 057 MWh remains unexplained. I found significant differences in the totals of planned maintenance hours for power stations between the two data sets provided to me by Eskom.)

Unit 6 accounted for 353 400 MWh of the combined planned maintenance figure. Using the official recorded total for planned maintenance, that left 177 657 MWh split over the three other units – which means they were running and not in cold reserve, as Eskom rules specifically prohibit work on units placed in available cold reserve because they might be needed at any time. As 520 212 MWh was placed in cold reserve, that left 166 812 MWh of available cold reserve hours split over four units.

The data shows that units were placed in cold reserve for anywhere between 5 and 16 hours – mostly after a planned outage, predominantly for boiler tube leak repairs – and that the reason many of the planned outages at Kriel were ended was because the units were placed in cold reserve – as opposed to returning to 'operation', which would have meant they were running. I believe the units taken offline for planned maintenance were placed in cold reserve *before* the maintenance was completed.

To my mind, 'ending' the outage early and placing the unit in cold reserve while the work is wrapped up is a neat way to effectively hide 520 212 MWh of repairs for unplanned breakdowns – because, booked as cold reserve, it does not count towards EAF because, technically, cold reserve means the unit is available.

If we conclude that the units were placed in cold reserve to achieve this purpose, how does this affect Kriel's overall performance for the month?

First, the official data – EAF of 66.53 per cent, PCLF of 25.05 per cent, UCLF of 7.66 per cent, OCLF of 0.76 per cent, GLF of 35.85 per cent and EUF, the crucial one, of 53.89 per cent. But when the cold reserve losses are factored in, EAF drops to 41.99 per cent, UCLF increases to 32.19 per cent and EUF rockets up to 85.37 per cent. If similar practices took place at the other coal-fired stations, it is understandable why unplanned breakdowns are significantly higher today than during Koko's tenure, particularly in the context of no load shedding and no significant expenditure on open cycle gas turbines to meet peak demand in 2016 and 2017. Unplanned losses at the legacy stations increased by 8 per cent, from 12.9 per cent in 2017/18 to 21.2 per cent in 2018/19, long before the arrival of De Ruyter, whom Koko now accuses of incompetence.

The effect on EAF at the legacy stations is also telling – in 2016/17, Eskom officially recorded an EAF for these stations of 75.01 per cent, a significant increase over the 67.7 per cent the year before. In 2017/18, Eskom recorded an EAF of 74.64 per cent for the legacy stations. This dropped to 67.75 per cent in 2018/19, mostly due to a high UCLF.

When the cold reserve losses are factored in, however, EAF drops by 1.77 per cent in 2016/17 and 3.34 per cent in 2017/18, to 73.24 and 71.3 per cent respectively. This is still an improvement on previous years and could, in my view, be explained by the impact of the card system and a real reduction in partial load losses at several power stations.

I also examined Eskom's other explanation for the improved performance during this time: the introduction of new capacity from Medupi, Kusile, Ingula and IPPs, which helped ease system constraints. It is true that the new builds increased capacity. One 720 MW unit at Medupi came online in September 2015 and contributed two million MWh to the grid from start-up to the end of April 2016. (Koko has repeatedly claimed that he and Brian Molefe stopped load shedding in August 2015.) Stage 1 load shedding is implemented when Eskom runs just 1 000 MW short of meeting demand, meaning that unit alone contributed significantly to preventing load shedding.

In July 2016, the first 331 MW unit at the Ingula pumped storage scheme came online. It was followed by two more units in September, assisting Eskom with 993 MW during peak periods to stave off load shedding.

The following year, 2017, saw another unit at Medupi and the first unit at Kusile come online in May and September respectively.

Yet the data shows that Eskom produced exactly the same amount of electricity in 2016, 2017 and 2018 (218 million MWh) despite having increased capacity of 21 million MWh.

Furthermore, 218 million MWh was not sufficient to meet demand, which at the time hovered around 235 million MWh per year on average. Instead of making up some of this shortfall with the cheaper coal-fired units that were in cold reserve and meant to be available for call-up, or even running the open cycle gas turbines to meet some of the peak demand, Eskom increased the amount spent procuring electricity from IPPs.

In 2016/17, Eskom's spend on IPP electricity increased by R6 billion to R21 billion for 11 million MWh – R2.5 billion of which was paid to the expensive IPP open cycle gas turbine peaking power plants Avon and Dedisa, for just 67 000 MWh of electricity.[18] Peaking power plants, also known as peakers, are generally run only when demand is higher than anticipated.

In 2017/18, the year in which Eskom placed 10 million MWh of coal units on cold reserve because there was 'surplus capacity', the utility paid R19 billion to IPPs for nine million MWh – R2.6 billion of which went to the Avon and Dedisa peakers for just 105 000 MWh of power.[19]

Eskom had no choice but to pay these considerable amounts to Avon and Dedisa due to minimum purchase requirements and capacity payments contained in power purchase agreements apparently negotiated by the national energy department and signed in 2013. Eskom was effectively the middleman.

For the other IPPs, however, it seems no such minimum requirements existed.

For two years, Koko refused to sign power purchase agreements with IPPs that had successfully bid to be part of the programme, delaying the introduction of an estimated 3 000 MW to 4 000 MW of new capacity by years. At the time, he said it was because they were too expensive comparatively.

'We told them that IPPs are expensive and that is why we refused to sign them. They pushed us out. Now that the matter is before the courts they are trying to manoeuvre themselves out of the mess we warned them about,' Koko tweeted on 18 February 2019.[20]

In response to a follow-up question over when exactly he began refusing to sign with IPPs, Koko tweeted: 'I refused to sign since June 2015. Hadebe signed them on 4 April 2018. He made a big blunder by signing them.'[21]

Yet the cost of electricity from IPPs has reduced significantly over the years as the technology has become cheaper to install and the market has become more competitive.

A senior Eskom official, who asked to remain anonymous, told me that Koko's refusal to timeously sign power purchase agreements with successful IPP bidders had contributed to the higher levels of load shedding since 2019. 'The new capacity would have come onboard by now. Even if it is reality that the IPPs are expensive, we should have sacrificed that for security of supply. Look at the cost of load shedding to the economy and compare that with what we could have paid for power from these newer, cheaper IPPs,' this official said.[22]

A recent Nova Economics study, commissioned by Eskom, found that one day of stage 1 load shedding – the loss of just 1 000 MW capacity – costs the economy R235.5 million, while a day of stage 2 load shedding (2 000 MW) costs R471.3 million.[23]

'The increase in unplanned losses [starting in early 2018] has many contributing factors,' Eskom said in response to questions around our investigation. 'The fact that it is an ageing fleet, run exceptionally "hard" for over 10 years, whilst performance improvement and reliability maintenance (such as mid-life refurbishment) was deferred due to capacity (due to the late decision by government to allow Eskom to build new plants) and funding (due to NERSA allowed revenue below prudent and efficient costs) are indeed major contributors to the decline in the performance of the Generation fleet.'

Much of what is in this chapter I reported for News24 in October 2021. It was split over three articles, the first of which was published on

25 October. Because the issues were so complex, News24 also published an explainer article, detailing five key takeaways from the investigation.

Koko challenged this explainer on two narrow aspects, neither of which related to the substance of our investigation. In December 2021, the Deputy Press Ombud dismissed his complaint and he promptly appealed. During oral arguments before a panel of representatives chaired by retired judge Bernard Ngoepe in March 2022, Koko accused me of racism. He said the only reason my reporting portrayed him in a negative light was because I could not stand the fact that two white men, De Ruyter and Oberholzer, were not achieving the same level of success as he had at Eskom. For all his arguments, Koko never once challenged the substance of my reporting in the in-depth pieces – that his card system had potentially driven power station staff to hide unplanned breakdowns – beyond his original denial, which I reported along with my findings.

But in April 2022, the appeals panel ruled that News24 had to retract two key statements in the explainer article. The first was that an increase in planned maintenance in 2015 was not sustained during Koko's tenure – the panel ordered News24 to clarify that this statement was not based on Eskom's audited financial statements and that the increase was, according to Eskom's annual financial statements, sustained.

The second – to the extent that the article gave the impression that continuing breakdowns at Eskom are attributable to Koko – the appeals panel ruled that such a statement was not justified and was unfair, and ordered News24 to retract it.

Koko had also complained about statements in the article that, during his tenure, there were 'damaging practices of running power generation units hard'. This complaint was rejected.

Koko's complaint, which was ultimately upheld by the appeals panel, centred on one paragraph in a body of work spanning approximately 9 000 words of reporting – the majority of which stands unchallenged.

The day after the ruling was handed down, Koko took to Twitter. He mischaracterised the ruling as proof that all the reporting about him had been labelled fake news by Judge Ngoepe, which is untrue. He even went a step further, labelling me and my editor, Pieter du Toit, 'blatant racists'. Attached to this tweet was a picture of Judge Ngoepe and a purported quote from the ruling, into which Koko had inserted words that were never part of the ruling – the names of Jan Oberholzer and André de Ruyter.

That same day, Judge Ngoepe and the panel directed Koko to remove his tweets, particularly the one showing the misquoted ruling. In a second directive, he was instructed to apologise to the appeals panel within three days, failing which News24 would not be called on to publish the corrections. According to the directive, he was to specifically indicate in his apology that he had inserted the names and lumped quotes from different parts of the ruling together without any indication that they did not follow on from one another. He removed the tweets, apologised to Ngoepe and the appeals committee, and News24 duly published the corrective statement.[24] To me, it was crucial in supporting the self-regulation of the media to comply with the sanction imposed by the appeals panel, even though I disagreed.

The paragraph Koko had complained about in the explainer had been selectively drawn from a caption on a graph in the main article – a valuable lesson for me as a journalist, but a fact that makes the decision by the appeals panel even more frustrating. In my opinion, events during Koko's tenure played a role in the increased unreliability the power stations face today, but in his hands, the appeals ruling became an instrument to misrepresent what News24 reported. In commenting on the ruling, emeritus professor and senior scholar at the Power Futures Lab at the University of Cape Town's Graduate School of Business Anton Eberhard argued that 'neither Eskom's annual auditing process, nor the judge presiding over the press case, were sufficiently exposed to technical details that showed how manipulation of the data might have been possible'.[25] Listening to Koko's submissions to the panel, and then witnessing his later misrepresentation of the ruling, has left me with the firm impression that he has a somewhat casual relationship with the truth.

I still have not found all the answers and every so often I find myself staring at row upon row of data in an Excel sheet, looking at our power stations through a strange prism of numbers so far removed from the roar of the turbines as to be part of another world. And I keep coming back to just one fact. In March 2018, the month after Koko resigned from Eskom, unplanned losses spiked to 16.5 per cent from 11.4 per cent in February. By November that year, the figure had breached 21 per cent. In 2021, unplanned breakdowns stood at 20 per cent. Add to that 12 per cent of planned maintenance and an extensive reliability maintenance programme and Eskom suffered the worst year of load shedding in its history.

13

'We would like you to look after this place'

FOR THE PAST TWO YEARS, Professor Malegapuru Makgoba has held the unenviable position of board chairperson of Eskom. He assumed the role in early 2020, around the same time as De Ruyter arrived at the utility, although he has been a board member since 2018.

It was under his direction that the board navigated first the Dabengwa matter and later Tshitangano's allegations. He presides over an entity that is increasingly criticised and has faced repeated calls for his head as load shedding continues to plague the country.[1] But the level of pushback that Makgoba and the board have faced, particularly over the hiring of two white men to run Eskom, has been visceral and deeply personal.

The fact that Oberholzer and De Ruyter are white has placed an additional burden on the board to prove they are not protecting them in any way, Makgoba told me in an interview in February 2022.[2]

Makgoba, an internationally recognised scientist and public health advocate, has received numerous awards, including a lifetime achievement award for the advancement of science from the National Research Foundation of South Africa and the Order of Mapungubwe for his work on developing science, democracy and higher education.[3] The full list of his achievements, honours, successes and travails are too many to mention but, most notably, he was the first black vice-chancellor of the University of the Witwatersrand, the first black chairperson and later president of the South African Medical Research Council, and a leading voice against the South African government's AIDS denialism. He was also vice-chancellor of the University of KwaZulu-Natal, one of the country's leading research institutions.

More recently, his report in his capacity as Health Ombud into the Life Esidimeni tragedy has been widely praised. The horrific scandal involved the deaths of an estimated 144 people with mental illnesses at psychiatric facilities in Gauteng from causes including mistreatment, starvation and neglect. The patients had been moved from state-run facilities to non-governmental organisations, many of which were not licensed to properly look after the people placed in their care.[4]

Makgoba is, by all accounts, a remarkable South African. He has travelled the globe and has an exceptionally incisive view of the country and the world. But, he agreed, Eskom was still an 'eye-opener'. He was part of the new board chaired by Jabu Mabuza and appointed by Zuma in early 2018, apparently after Ramaphosa and then public enterprises minister Lynne Brown had sufficiently impressed on the president the need for dramatic change at Eskom.[5]

'For me the excitement was being in this environment that I have never been, seeing it as a challenge from which I could learn, and develop my own understanding of leadership, because I had come from a very academic life – protected, ethical, clear boundaries where you understand you don't cross these, you don't do that,' Makgoba told me.[6]

Armed with an SIU proclamation, Mabuza made it clear from the start that they would root out those Eskom officials who were doing business with the utility. The SIU identified 5 452 Eskom officials who had not submitted declaration of interest forms, and 324 staff members who were doing business with the utility, in some cases through companies indirectly linked to them. Of the 324, 135 had received payments from Eskom, 99 were referred for disciplinary action and at least 15 were referred by the SIU to the National Prosecuting Authority for criminal prosecution.[7]

It is not often highlighted, but there are serious strides being made at the utility in addressing widespread corruption. The big contracts that make the headlines are an important part of that. But there is no doubt that the clean-up operation has caused a deluge of ill-feeling towards

De Ruyter and Makgoba, who are leading the charge with the steadfast assistance of Oberholzer and chief financial officer Calib Cassim.

Their detractors claim they are incompetent. The reality is they are rolling a giant boulder uphill, battling against well-entrenched patronage networks, the most ruthless of which – the coal suppliers and transporters – is yet to be fully uprooted. What has come before will pale in comparison to that fight. Equally important is an investigation into diesel suppliers, which will be no less daunting.

Makgoba understands this very clearly. The attacks won't be stopping any time soon. It's something he thought about when he took the position of board chair.

'The minister called me and told me the president would call me. I think Cyril [Ramaphosa] said to me, you know that Jabu has left, and we thought that in the interests of the board, we would like you to look after this place. Those, I can remember, those were the words, just to look after this place,' Makgoba recalled.[8]

He accepted, he explained, because he had seen the problems and felt he could tackle them: 'I was quite clear in my mind that the problems of Eskom were deeply systemic and they couldn't be approached in a sort of linear fashion, and they couldn't be approached in a manner where you fail to understand that Eskom is a system. It's a company, but its design and its role in the country is entrenched and systematic ... You just have to appreciate when load shedding occurs, the ripple effect is across everywhere. Across the nation. Whilst economists worry about the money, people worry about their livelihood, and this is often forgotten. It is the well-being and the livelihood [people worry about].'

He provided an example: One day during load shedding, he was trying to open his garage door and, in the process, hurt his shoulder. It occasioned a doctor's visit and a shoulder that still troubles him today. The ripple effects were endless, he said.

'I identified really that the problem of this company is systemic; therefore its solution requires a systemic approach,' he told me. 'That was the first thing I had identified. The second issue I had identified was that – and I had not only identified it at Eskom but also in my career – boards or councils in South Africa, because of the newness of how they are now constituted, boards or councils fail to understand the roles between themselves and management. There is often an overreach of board control over management. But at the same time, when there are problems, they distance themselves and say, no, it's management problems. The same thing you find in government that when something positive comes, government takes the credit, but when there is a problem, the board takes the blame.'

According to Makgoba, to move forward from a good governance perspective, Eskom had to recognise that executive management was there to tackle operational issues, while the board was there to conduct oversight and strategic direction.

He never had any doubts, however, that it would be difficult.

'I told my relatives that whenever there was load shedding, my ears would start to itch because everybody would be swearing at me ... but it's fine. I get lots of phone calls, sometimes compliments, sometimes anger. On the whole, I understand people's anger ... and I respect that. What I am determined to do is to make sure, first of all, we don't fall back to where we were, but more importantly, I think, the institution or organisation begins to move in a trajectory where it begins to understand itself.

'At some stage or another, when you look and see what was happening at Eskom, it was like a jungle. It was everyone for themselves. There was a caucus here, and they would pick it up and in the same time in the process of picking it up, there were disagreements between people – the organisation was not cohesive, they don't have that spirit, that we are one organisation, we have a role to play. These are issues that are simple but need to be there in an organisation that has so much influence.'

As mentioned, Makgoba has endured significant criticism for De Ruyter's appointment. He was part of the team that interviewed prospective CEOs and he stands by the decision, saying that De Ruyter was the best choice.

'One of the things in South Africa that sometimes I find very difficult is how racism or the pressures of racism play a part, I think even in areas where they should not,' he told me.

Makgoba provided an analogy: When he chaired the Rhodes Scholarship committee for the KwaZulu-Natal region, there were always big debates over representation, equity and empowerment. As chairperson, he said, he made it clear that the scholarships were about merit.

'Meritocracy, you know? And if we start fiddling around with the criteria for meritocracy and bring other new adjectives into it, we are going to find it very difficult to know whether who we are selecting are the best or not. It went down very well with the committee. I said to them, you know we are going to encounter here lots of white students, young people that are bright, which whether you go to the Freedom Charter or the Constitution, South Africa belongs to them, and they need to be given opportunities, and whether we are going to then put an element of saying how do we then address the history of the past, but I said to them, if we want to redress the past, we need to redress it with the people who meet the criteria.'

The danger, he said, is that if you attempt to redress the past with people who do not meet the criteria, you are setting them up for failure.

'I was quite clear that when we were selecting someone for Eskom, that was the criteria I was going to champion. Whoever is the best for this country because we are talking about a national project here, we are not talking about my project or anything like that, it's a national project. And if we find the best person, I think we must defend that against the pressure. The pressure will come. But we must be ready to defend it, and that was how I looked at it. And it came immediately.'

In Makgoba's view, selecting people on popular sentiment is a problem South Africa has yet to overcome: 'I used to say to people, if you want the chief of the defence force, don't call me to become one. Even if people were to march for me, I would refuse, because I know nothing about the army, I have never even held a gun in my life, why should I be chief? Just because I have the majority of people behind me? It doesn't work like that. But how many people accept these kinds of positions?

'But we do this in South Africa so often, at many levels. And, of course, once you give people false power, and they themselves know they are not qualified, they mess up. They don't follow the rules because they were not appointed according to the rules. I spent enormous time speaking to the minister as to why André should be appointed.'

Ramaphosa and Gordhan, too, have come under fire for the selection.

'They are under pressure, not because there is a criterion, they are under pressure because of the social system,' Makgoba told me. 'What I do tell people often is that the public has its demands. We who are leaders have a role to teach the public what is right. If you invest in the right thing, it is in the interest of the public. If you invest in the wrong thing because of the public, you are also destroying the future of the public. We have, I suppose, a very enviable position, to stand up for the things that are unpopular but in the long-term interest of the country.'

But the pressures Makgoba faces are fundamentally different from the ones faced by De Ruyter.

'It is a very difficult thing because you are called a traitor, you have abandoned your people. You are either, you have now joined, you have a little bit of money, you think you don't belong there; all these things will come. But at the end of the day, deep down, in people's hearts, they know that if you do something in the interest of the public, because you have thought about it, you know it will stand the test of time and it will be in the best interest. And that has been something I really feel very strongly about. I subscribe to the view that South Africa belongs to all who live in it, blacks and whites, and they should be given the opportunities that are there,' he explained.

'This whole issue of having two white males running Eskom, it is a big issue in the country. We might not talk about it as much ... but what people forget is that these are South Africans. These are people committed to a national asset of the country. And these are people who have been appointed, by black people. The board that appointed André was largely black people. So, what do they think of this board that appointed them? They think that these are not Africans? It's an insult on that level, it's a deep insult, that you can appoint a board, you give it a mandate, they appoint a CEO, and then you start thinking that they somehow belong somewhere else.'

The Dabengwa debacle started soon after Makgoba assumed the position of chair. He explained that Dabengwa was seen as a valuable contributor to the board, which he said lacked engineering expertise. Dabengwa's allegations that De Ruyter had misled them 'came as a surprise' to Makgoba. 'On the face of it, it looked ridiculous,' he told me.

Life has taught Makgoba that when someone acts in this way, there is usually something else happening – De Ruyter's decision to move towards cancelling the fuel oil tender must have been causing 'pain' elsewhere, he said. But that was not the ambit of the investigation, Makgoba reiterated. Appointing Trengove to examine Dabengwa's allegations were at the latter's insistence that the investigation could not be undertaken by the board, which he claimed was biased. 'Whatever [Dabengwa] might say, we did what he requested us to do: he wanted an independent process, we gave it to him. He had been given an opportunity to give his side of the story,' Makgoba told me.

While the battle between De Ruyter and Dabengwa raged, and later when Tshitangano made his claims of racism and nepotism, the board and Eskom were busy with other matters. They were 'never paralysed', Makgoba said. The unbundling of the utility – into three entities, for generation, transmission and distribution – had to go ahead without delay.

'I can say this with confidence now, today we hear about the change in electricity regulation to set up this new company [the National Transmission Company], it is because of the work that Eskom has done and it's because of the work that André committed himself to do,' Makgoba told me unequivocally. 'The fuel oil thing, Econ Oil, it has gone through the courts, now we are vindicated, despite what Advocate Cassim said, we have been vindicated in the whole thing, it was correct to address that matter of Econ Oil. It has been addressed through the courts, independent of us, and we have gone onto the right path.'

Successive court judgments in Eskom's favour – the High Court setting aside the tender award and later denying leave to appeal, as well as the Supreme Court of Appeal denying an application by Econ Oil – vindicated both the utility and its CEO.

But for Dabengwa and De Ruyter, there could be no reconciliation.

Makgoba said De Ruyter did not have to tell him that either he or Dabengwa had to go: 'You fight with the chair of the board or you fight with the CEO, and you are a member of the board, whatever the circumstances are, you can't work together. You have destroyed trust, you have destroyed the relationship, you can't be brought back, there is no mediation or political solution to that. Especially when you have involved the law, you can only deal with it if you sit together and talk, once you have a legal document that has investigated everything and it's going to be in the public domain, you are finished.'

During the course of our interview, Makgoba revealed that, in his opinion, there were members of the board who did 'not necessarily agree' with De Ruyter's appointment as CEO.

'It may have been the instigator, to find something wrong with this person,' Makgoba speculated. 'If you couldn't get it through the board in the appointment, you can get it by finding fault with the appointee very soon. It was a tactic, a wrangling.'

How much does it distract from the urgent business of the board when the CEO and COO are constantly under attack?

'The board has always been solidly behind the executive management,' Makgoba affirmed. 'We had to deal with Jan, you know how many investigations he had, even more than André. The pressure to investigate is not necessarily what the board wants to do, but it is the pressure to deal with the public perception, and I think this is what Advocate Cassim misunderstood, it was not in our best interest to investigate André, but we had to clear the public perception that here was a white folk who was being protected and not investigated when complaints are lodged.'

Makgoba told me that every issue De Ruyter has identified for attention has been spot on so far. The board is comfortable, he insisted, and continues to support the CEO and his team: 'I think we have to compliment him for staying, despite all the winds that have been blowing for him to get out. The bottom line is the relationship between the board and André is very strong. And the relationship between the board and the shareholder and André is also very good. At the moment I think I can say Eskom is in a honeymoon, because it has got relationships at its governance level that are all aligned.'

Any kind of breakdown in these relationships would 'create panic and anxiety that would filter through the organisation', Makgoba added.

I asked if the criticism was something he had learned to live with.

'I have lived my life in the past 25 years being criticised,' he replied. 'When I was at the Medical Research Council, I was criticised, when I was at Wits, when I was at the University of KwaZulu-Natal. I have never lived life without criticism, but it has made me stronger and appreciate maybe that what I do matters to people, otherwise they wouldn't say what they are saying. I am humbled by that, it's often not pleasant, but sometimes I understand why people make the criticisms they do.

'I do get angry but maybe my medical training helps me not to get too empathetic to issues, I just detach myself and say what really needs to be done. People say to me you are a medical doctor not an engineer, you shouldn't be at Eskom. I often tell them, if you are working at Eskom, it's like working in an ICU, you have to have the eye of anticipation. Many people at Eskom don't anticipate, they react. And that culture has not yet taken place. But you can't teach people anticipation.

'I suppose it's like, many people eat food, but we don't know what is in the kitchen. Some of us suffer from the fact that we are in the kitchen, while others just wait for the plate. It's just the nature of life, when you are eating the food, it's not the same as the person who cooks it, or the person who has to look after the vegetables, whether they have cleaned it all properly or not.

'The emotional baggage of apartheid and history are sometimes just too much in South Africa. Sometimes when you go overseas and you see how things are being run and how things are happening, you think, when is it going to happen in my country? But as soon as you get back, you understand.'

14

'Did I mention the debt?'

OBERHOLZER ESTIMATED THAT, AT ONE point, he was spending 40 per cent of his time just responding to investigations, digging through old documents and emails, speaking to other Eskom officials, getting clarity and drafting reports.

'That's probably right,' De Ruyter said of his own battles. 'The impact on my and his effectiveness is enormous. Remember when Jan was investigated, I had to investigate him. I wrote the report that went to the board that eventually resulted in his exoneration. So now I am sitting on a Saturday writing a report.'[1]

Despite this, De Ruyter defended the board, explaining that the boards of SOEs have an incredibly difficult job. In the private sector, the board can study the allegation and say they believe it has no merit or substance, and decline to investigate.

'But because Eskom is so in the public eye and because it is so subject to scrutiny, the board has to bend over and really exert itself to demonstrate that it has turned over every stone, particularly given the history of state capture,' De Ruyter explained. 'So, when it came to the Solly Tshitangano thing, I was actually the person who was saying, let's have an inquiry. I need to clear my name. And for as long as Solly is out there making these allegations and he is being entertained by a significant portion of the media, including SABC and IOL, then I will always be under a cloud. So let's clear the air.'

Eskom is still facing enormous challenges. Yet despite the constant attacks and problems over the past two years, both Oberholzer and De Ruyter appear determined to see it through.

Oberholzer has a tough choice ahead of him – in 2023 he will turn 65 and will be eligible for pension. But he does not see himself stopping work. Possibly, he told me, he will focus on identifying successors and passing on as much as possible of his institutional knowledge before departing. 'If you ask my wife, she will tell you she is not looking forward to the day when I have to sit at home,' he laughed. 'I have to be busy, I can't just sit still.'

The job of chief operations officer at Eskom is one of the most challenging positions in the country. 'Every night when I put my head on the pillow I then say, have I made a positive contribution today to the lives of 60 million people? That is what is nagging me. I love it, I really love it.'

But, he conceded, he usually has to reflect on immensely tough days as the operational challenges of a damaged and ageing system catch up with him. 'I take the responsibility that I have to the country extremely serious,' Oberholzer said. 'And I am a perfectionist, when you talk to my wife she will tell you what a pain in the backside this guy is, but that's just the way my creators put me together. You know, when God said, tomorrow I am going to give out patience, I wasn't there, because I didn't get the email. I am a very impatient person, you can say it is a weakness or a strength, I am sure a lot of people who are working with me say it's a weakness, but it doesn't matter.'[2]

De Ruyter, in comparison, is 10 years younger than Oberholzer and could be earning far more money in the private sector. Recently, an Eskom official told me that De Ruyter accepted a pay cheque that is 20 per cent less than that of his predecessor, Hadebe, and that he gets no benefits – no medical aid, no pension, no allowances, no bonuses. In the private sector, CEO bonuses are highly valued incentives to ensure good company performance.

He shrugged when I asked him about this. 'It's not something I talk about often,' he said.

There is another concern, though – who will take over from De Ruyter when he eventually leaves? Who wants to become the head of a troubled

'DID I MENTION THE DEBT?'

SOE, where they will be maligned in the media for every problem, be accused of racism or corruption in attempts to get rid of them, and face off against political interference and patronage networks that are becoming increasingly desperate to maintain their stranglehold on the purse strings?

De Ruyter has few years left to earn good money in the private sector – and if the right opportunity comes knocking that will remove him and his family from the public eye, how hard would it be to convince him to go, to leave a job where he works too hard for too little? Why he has stayed this long is mystifying.

He attributes it to a sense of national duty, comparing the job to a second national service. 'It is sometimes very frustrating, and exhausting. It's a job of Sisyphean proportions and Sisyphean complexity.'

A senior Eskom official with whom I spoke was more blunt. 'National service is fine, but it also shouldn't be the Charge of the Light Brigade. It shouldn't be an exercise in self-immolation on the altar of national interest,' this person said, referencing the constant attacks.[3]

Oberholzer similarly related unpleasant experiences linked to the public allegations: 'It becomes hard when your son tells you about how another student at university came up to him and said, *Jou pa is lekker skelm, nè? Hoeveel het hy gesteel?* [Your father is very dodgy. How much did he steal?] It's hard when some family members refuse to speak to you any more [because they believe what is written in the newspapers].'

Both men have also faced increasing threats to their personal safety. In late 2021, Eskom opened a case of intimidation against a suspected EFF member who posted on Twitter that De Ruyter and his family should be confronted at their home. He recently got bodyguards for the first time.

Oberholzer takes a pragmatic approach to the threats. 'I sat the whole family down and spoke to them, and said, listen, this is the reality. And they all said to me, you do your job, you do what's right,' he explained. However, should the day come when one of them asks him to leave Eskom, if they feel it is becoming too unsafe, he will pack his things and leave immediately. 'But they will never do that,' he added.

According to De Ruyter, the greatest challenges facing Eskom remain security of electricity supply, continued restructuring and unbundling.

'What we have done with transmission is actually a massive achievement. To do this in the private sector is a huge deal. It's an enormous thing, and we have just sort of done it on the side. Delivering on that is very important,' he explained to me.

In late 2021, Eskom announced that it had established a legal entity, the National Transmission Company, which would absorb the transmission division's assets and liabilities. In early 2022, De Ruyter explained at a media briefing that one of the final hurdles was getting express permission from the lenders to unbundle the power utility, which was under way.

'The securing of the funds, R131 billion, I think that was a big milestone, but now to successfully translate that into 10 000 kilometres of new transmission line, expanding the distribution grid, putting in place some modest renewable energy generation capacity for Eskom, enabling the just energy transition, those are huge challenges,' De Ruyter told me.

The R131 billion is made up of loans and grants from those wealthier countries that were part of the 2021 United Nations Climate Change Conference (COP26) and is aimed at enabling a move away from coal generation, which has ensured that Eskom is today the world's worst polluter among power companies.

'We have in the past spoken and said a lot about the transition away from coal, and we did not have the financing option needed available to us, but this really gives the country an opportunity to decisively pivot to a new future,' De Ruyter told Fin24 in early November 2021, adding that new coal or nuclear generation projects could not be built fast enough even if Eskom had the money.[4]

'Did I mention the debt?' De Ruyter asked me.

By negotiating better terms on older debt, he has managed to reduce Eskom's overall debt burden, which will at the end of the 2022 financial year stand at around R400 billion.

He also mentioned tariffs and the battle to make Eskom financially sustainable. He pointed out that arguably the country's greatest period of industrialisation, driven by the pioneer Hendrik van der Bijl, was marked with alignment of policy and practice. Comparatively, the situation today does not enable any great strides in industrialisation, and he gave an example: the punitive import duty on electric vehicles.

'There is no local industry to protect, so why the tariff?' he asked me rhetorically. 'Unless you have demand, the industry won't start. If there is sufficient local demand, the industry will kick off eventually, because the numbers will just make sense. And again, it comes back to this enabling environment, where everything is not a struggle. Where I don't need to write to National Treasury and say please help me with municipal debt.'

A lack of smart policy and integration of policy, he said, is holding Eskom back.

'For it to be doable, I think if Eskom is indeed the greatest threat to the national economy, if it is indeed the greatest brake on development and growth, then let's elevate it, and let's, you know, I don't want to use a military metaphor, but let's make this a national priority, and let's fix it,' he said.

De Ruyter's level of frustration, he told me, is huge. But if he did not tackle what he perceives as major obstacles piecemeal, he would get nowhere 'and I would have had a stroke'. Yet, he added, 'I see the opportunity; I see the positive things that can happen. And I see the goodwill of the Western world to make money available to us and believe me there is still a lot of goodwill out there.'

What De Ruyter did not mention, however, was that the policy changes need to come from forward-thinking and progressive politicians. Gwede Mantashe, the minister of energy and mineral resources, is determined to cling to coal, diametrically at odds with basically the entire world.

'Coal is growing, it is generating revenue for the fiscus, it is doing well,' Mantashe said during a keynote address at an energy summit convened by the South African Youth Economic Council in Johannesburg in November 2021. 'Now, what do we do with it? Do we set it alight and destroy it? My argument is that let's allow it to benefit [South Africa] as long as it can.'[5]

Business Day reported that Mantashe refused to attend COP26 in Glasgow because, he said, 'many people will be frightened' or even ask why a 'coal fundamentalist' is there. Speaking of the just energy transition (the transition to a low-carbon economy), he said: 'It must protect livelihoods. To me just transition is a term. Just transition is a transition from high carbon emissions to low carbon emissions. Others say it's a transition to renewables. But I say: "no, no, it's a transition from high carbon emissions to low carbon emissions."

'This thing of saying destroy coal quickly is second to Nongqawuse … a prophet who said we must kill all our cattle and we will be rich. We are still waiting for those riches.

'I'm saying, you don't destroy what you have on the basis of hope that something better is coming. You build on what you know and what you have.'[6]

During the same address, he pointed to South Africa's commitment to renewable energy through the independent power producer programme. But one industry insider explained that Mantashe's attitude is a middle finger to countries who want to help South Africa address energy concerns while at the same time reduce pollution. 'Gwede is basically telling them, f-you. Take your money and f-off,' this person told me.[7]

Mantashe is also facing criticism over his comments for another reason – they are directly opposed to his own government's policy, namely the integrated resource plan, the latest version of which was approved in 2019 and calls for the decommissioning of 35 000 of the current 40 000 MW of coal generation capacity over which Eskom presides. The plan specifies that the replacement capacity should come from renewable projects, such as wind and solar generation.

In January 2022, *The Economist* reported that little has happened to start this process 'largely because of resistance from mining unions, populists and politicians who have grown rich selling overpriced coal to Eskom'.[8]

'Mr Mantashe may well stand with Ramaphosa against the pro-corruption wing of the ANC – as he did in 2017 – though some pundits reckon he may also be considering knifing the president to make his own run for power. In either case he will want the backing of the country's two main industrial trade unions, representing miners and metalworkers, which between them muster some 650,000 members. Both unions back coal, a big export, and have opposed renewable power, which has become a touchstone for the political left: Floyd Shivambu, a leader of the populist Economic Freedom Fighters party, thinks renewable energy is "a colonial takeover engineered by the West",' *The Economist* reported.

The NUM has already indicated its support for Mantashe's determination for more coal projects.

'The goodwill is there, I promise you,' De Ruyter told me. 'I talk to foreign governments. Honestly, it's not about recolonising us. It is still about helping us. There is such an opportunity that we have got right here, but there is a finite pot of money, but if we mess this up, it's going to go somewhere else.'

An energy sector expert, who asked not to be identified, explained it to me as follows: 'Politicians sitting in these wealthy countries, for example France, get reports from all over the world – South Africa, Vietnam. And this minister has a budget, and his or her goal is to spend this money on projects that will make them look good and improve their chances for re-election, meaning there is a time pressure element to the investment decision. In South Africa, there is risk. And internally we don't have our shit together, with the president saying one thing and Mantashe saying another. And there is a strong risk the money will be misappropriated to projects designed with kickbacks in mind. So, the politician looks at Indonesia, and sees they do have their shit together. They've got good governance; they are lining up to share their plans.'[9]

South Africa, this expert explained, is on the cusp of an opportunity to reignite tangible growth. Our record high unemployment, stagnant economy, and huge financial, economic, social and political risks can all be addressed through job creation: 'How do you get them jobs? Not by legislating it, but by creating conditions that are conducive for investors. And also by getting regulation in place that is smart and effective, not brute force regulation that makes investors privately say, what the fuck are you guys thinking?'

De Ruyter and Eskom, however, do not make policy. They must focus on the job at hand while the bunfight over access to the R131 billion in funding goes on and the power stations we do have continue to pollute and break down, costing many millions of rands to fix and keep running.

Epilogue

Eskom has a long history, filled equally with aspiration and glory as with corruption and decay. Most South Africans groan audibly when the state power utility is mentioned. The majority, who live in poverty in crime-ridden areas, receive no basic services. We are a society that is thoroughly fed up with our government's inadequate performance.

We are not alone. South Africa is unique in a number of ways, but it is depressingly akin to countries the world over where many live forgotten between election cycles, where promises are made and broken, over and over again. And no promise is bigger than the right to safety and security. Electricity, that mundane flick of the switch, is a cornerstone of that right.

The ANC-led government has neglected its principles in caring for the poor. In the face of the largesse and luxury afforded by their well-paid political positions, the party's leaders have forgotten the desperation, ideals and struggle that gave birth to their movement.

The South African economy is on life support – it has been for years. There can be no debate that the provision of electricity is critical if there is to be any hope of even partially resurrecting it. Rightly or wrongly, Eskom is currently the main provider of electricity in the country and, as such, there can be no further delays in addressing the problems that have plagued the entity for decades. Eskom should be the first thing our leaders think of in the morning and the last thing they think of at night, because Eskom is a national disaster and it is time that we all started treating it as such.

It needs support, both political and moral. It needs money. But most of all, its leaders need the space and understanding to grapple with the problems and find the solutions to pull Eskom, and the country, back from the brink of disaster. This does not mean they should get a free pass. If there is wrongdoing, it should be called out. If there are mistakes, they should be highlighted. But we should no longer simply call for heads to roll every time there is a power cut. There are factors at play beyond the control of André de Ruyter, Jan Oberholzer, Calib Cassim, Malegapuru Makgoba, Phillip Dukashe and Segomoco Scheppers, who deserve our praise to equal our ire.

They are undertaking tough jobs in the worst of circumstances. They cannot win against the avalanche unless they know we are with them – not accusing without evidence, not believing every accusation simply because it is made and, most importantly, not judging their abilities on the colour of their skin. There are many good people at the utility who continue to work extremely hard and against all odds to keep the lights on and the industry working. Relief will come, but the country will have to endure a lot more pain before then.

Despite my cynical view that Eskom is the single biggest threat to South Africa's survival, De Ruyter, Oberholzer and Makgoba all impressed on me their own sense of hope.

De Ruyter was able to meet 'Mr Electricity', Dr Ian McRae, in 2020. McRae, considered by many to be a pioneer of the modern Eskom, was the company's CEO between 1985 and 1994.

I asked De Ruyter what advice McRae gave him.

'Importance of the power stations, focus on the people,' De Ruyter told me. 'But it was more important to see his passion and commitment, even at his advanced age – he passed away a few months after I met him. But it was a huge privilege to receive the spirit of the great Eskom from the man himself.'[1]

Oberholzer sees signs of hope on the horizon: 'I must admit to thinking sometimes, especially when it's tough and with all these attacks on myself, thinking what the hell am I taking this for? But it's very difficult when you are dealing with a system that was broken, and it was on purpose that it was broken. For me it's to get it in the right direction, and are we? After three and a half years, it seems – and I am comfortable saying – we are slowly but surely moving forward.'[2]

'Of course, there are still challenges here and there in the organisation, for example the culture in the organisation, it's a culture of the zoo, where people don't really understand they belong to an organisation of national importance and they need to operate and work in a certain way, and I think that's a big project we are now trying to undertake here as we are busy unbundling,' Makgoba told me. 'And then, of course, the issue of skills which everybody talks about. It's a very important thing because during the state capture years, skills have been lost and somehow or another we have to address that matter going forward. It has not been a waste of time, because despite all the things that have been happening, the organisation is now stable, it's much better. It's better focused on what it's supposed to be doing. I think if you go around, people are now alive to their responsibilities at Eskom. They are trying their best to do that. The operations are getting better, although maybe it has not yet translated into the elimination of load shedding, which is how people measure Eskom's performance, it's the only thing that matters.'[3]

Load shedding is the physical manifestation of Eskom's many problems. For us, it *is* the only thing that matters. It is worse now because real effort is being made to return power stations to a state of reliability, and to re-inject an ethos of accountability and purpose into the utility. It is these strides that Makgoba talks about that remain our greatest hope of achieving energy security and ending load shedding. But they cannot continue to make these strides if they are constantly under attack. If Eskom and the country are to ever move forward, the onslaught must end.

Acknowledgements

Thank you to my wonderful better half, Chantelle. Without your generous love, support, encouragement and the copious cups of coffee you make, this book would never have been possible. To Ms K and Mr R, this is for you, in the hope that one day the country of your birth will face challenges less serious. Thank you for putting up with my moaning and grumpiness as lack of sleep got the better of me.

Huge appreciation must be given to André de Ruyter and Jan Oberholzer, both of whom made time for my questions both personal and inane, and walked me through their challenges with good grace and humour. They had far more important things to do than speak with me, and I am grateful for their time. To the other Eskom people who helped, thank you. I can't name you here, but I am eternally grateful.

I must also thank Sarvam, who I believe is the busiest person in the world, for scheduling (and rescheduling) interviews.

To Marida Fitzpatrick, for cracking the whip and for planting the seed for this book, thank you for guiding this first-timer through the trenches of book writing. Thanks must also go to Robert Plummer and, of course, Bronwen Maynier, who made sense of my ramblings by beating this book into shape.

To my editors at News24, Pieter du Toit and Adriaan Basson, thank you for the time, space and guidance. And to Sipho Masondo, Azarrah Karrim and Jeff Wicks, the investigations team at News24, thank you.

To Edward, you rogue, the proceeds will in part be funding the purchase of new socks.

Last, but certainly not least, thank you to the thousands of Eskom employees who continue to work hard, sacrificing time away from their families, striving to keep the lights on as the edifice crumbles. I hope you will continue to remain steadfast, even while those of your colleagues concerned chiefly with scheming and stealing give you all a bad name.

Abbreviations

AFP: Agence France-Presse
ANC: African National Congress
BKS: Bruinette Kruger Stoffberg
CCMA: Commission for Conciliation, Mediation and Arbitration
CEO: chief executive officer
COO: chief operating officer
CPO: chief procurement officer
EAF: energy availability factor
EFF: Economic Freedom Fighters
EUF: energy utilisation factor
FFS: Fuel Firing Systems Refiners
GCEO: group chief executive officer
GLF: generation load factor
IFC: investment and finance committee
IPC: interim payment certificate
IPP: independent power producer
IRP: integrated resource plan
MW: megawatt
MWh: megawatt hour
NUM: National Union of Mineworkers
O&S: Sasol Olefins and Surfactants
OCLF: other capability loss factor
PCLF: planned capability loss factor
SAFTU: South African Federation of Trade Unions
SCOPA: Standing Committee on Public Accounts
SEC: Securities and Exchange Commission

SIU: Special Investigating Unit
SOE: state-owned enterprise
UCLF: unplanned capability loss factor
UNISA: University of South Africa
UP: University of Pretoria

Notes

Introduction
1. Cowan, K., 'Eskom finds evidence of sabotage at Lethabo Power Station – pylon supports were cut', *News24*, 19 November 2021. https://www.news24.com/news24/southafrica/investigations/eskomfiles/breaking-eskom-finds-evidence-of-sabotage-at-lethabo-power-station-pylon-supports-were-cut-20211119 as accessed on 17 December 2021.
2. Moatshe, R., 'Eskom load shedding last year worst since 2015', *Pretoria News*, 10 August 2021. https://www.iol.co.za/pretoria-news/news/eskom-load-shedding-last-year-worst-since-2015-51c03727-a763-4cf1-8bd6-b9d4e1f387fa as accessed on 19 November 2021.
3. Umraw, A., 'Eskom the "main theatre" for state capture: Jabu Mabuza', *TimesLIVE*, 22 February 2019. https://www.timeslive.co.za/politics/2019-02-22-eskom-the-main-theatre-for-state-capture-jabu-mabuza/ as accessed on 28 December 2021.
4. Author interview with André de Ruyter, 15 January 2022.
5. Author interview with Jan Oberholzer, 28 January 2022.
6. Author unknown, 'Millions spent on increasing security for Eskom's infrastructure paying off: Mantshantsha', *SABC*, 28 January 2022. https://www.sabcnews.com/sabcnews/millions-spent-on-increasing-security-for-eskoms-infrastructure-paying-off-mantshantsha/ as accessed on 30 January 2022.
7. Author unknown, 'NUM says Eskom lying over "sabotage" claims', *ENCA*, 18 June 2018. https://www.enca.com/south-africa/num-slams-eskom-over-sabotage-claims as accessed on 16 March 2022.
8. Khumalo, S. and Cronje, J., 'Ramaphosa: "There has been a measure of sabotage" behind power cuts', *Fin24*, 11 December 2019. https://www.news24.com/fin24/Economy/ramaphosa-there-has-been-a-measure-of-sabotage-behind-power-cuts-20191211 as accessed on 16 March 2022.
9. Cronje, J., 'NPA closes Eskom sabotage case, cites lack of evidence of foul play', *Fin24*, 29 December 2020. https://www.news24.com/fin24/companies/industrial/npa-closes-eskom-sabotage-case-cites-lack-of-evidence-of-foul-play-20201229 as accessed on 16 March 2022.
10. Cowan, K., Masondo, S. and Karrim, A., 'Fire, sabotage, and Treasury delays drove up Eskom's Majuba Rail costs from "R108m to R6.5bn"', *News24*, 20 September 2021. https://www.news24.com/news24/southafrica/investigations/eskomfiles/the-eskom-files-fire-sabotage-and-treasury-delays-drove-up-eskoms

-majuba-rail-costs-from-r108m-to-r65bn-20210920 as accessed on 16 March 2022.
11. Author interview with Jan Oberholzer, 28 January 2022.
12. Author unknown, 'Millions spent on increasing security for Eskom's infrastructure paying off: Mantshantsha', *SABC*, 28 January 2022. https://www.sabcnews.com/sabcnews/millions-spent-on-increasing-security-for-eskoms-infrastructure-paying-off-mantshantsha/ as accessed on 30 January 2022.
13. Davis, R., 'The man who blew up Koeberg', *Daily Maverick*, 31 October 2020. https://www.dailymaverick.co.za/article/2020-10-31-the-man-who-blew-up-koeberg/ as accessed on 16 March 2022.
14. Botha, N.J., 'The history, basis and current status of the right or duty to extradite in public international and South African law', thesis, University of South Africa, January 1992.
15. Davis, 'The man who blew up Koeberg'.
16. Author interview with André de Ruyter, 15 January 2022.

Chapter 1: The more things change, the more they stay the same

1. Various, *Beeld*, 1980 to 1988, Media24 archive.
2. Author interviews.
3. AFP, 'Government ignored Eskom pleas', *Fin24*, 12 December 2007. https://www.news24.com/fin24/goverment-ignored-eskom-pleas-20071212 as accessed on 16 March 2022.
4. Report by Jan Oberholzer, 21 June 2021, responding to an investigation by Crawford Independent Associate.
5. Steyn, L., 'Eskom runs up R1bn diesel bill in November', *Fin24*, 8 December 2021. https://www.news24.com/fin24/economy/eskom-runs-up-r1bn-diesel-bill-in-november-20211208 as accessed on 16 March 2022.
6. Steyn, G., 'Investment and uncertainty: Historical experience with power sector investment in South Africa and its implications for current challenges', working paper prepared for the Management Programme in Infrastructure Reform and Regulation (MIR) at the Graduate School of Business at the University of Cape Town, 15 March 2006. https://www.gsb.uct.ac.za/files/eskom-investmentuncertainty.pdf as accessed on 16 March 2022.
7. Ibid.
8. Author interview with Jan Oberholzer, 28 January 2022.
9. Reuters, 'We can't afford nuclear deal now, Ramaphosa tells Putin', *TimesLIVE*, 26 July 2018. https://www.timeslive.co.za/politics/2018-07-26-we-cant-afford-a-nuclear-deal-now-ramaphosa-tells-putin/ as accessed on 16 March 2022.
10. Masondo, S., Karrim, A. and Cowan, K., 'Over the brink: Data shows how Koko's Eskom seemingly cooked the electricity books', *News24*, 25 October 2021. https://www.news24.com/news24/southafrica/investigations/eskomfiles/the-eskom-files-over-the-brink-data-shows-how-kokos-eskom-seemingly-cooked-the-electricity-books-20211025 as accessed on 16 March 2022.
11. Merten, M., 'Increase to 100MW embedded generation threshold will give

"oomph" to South African economy, says Ramaphosa', *Daily Maverick*, 10 June 2021. https://www.dailymaverick.co.za/article/2021-06-10-increase-to-100mw-embedded-generation-threshold-will-give-oomph-to-south-african-economy-says-ramaphosa/ as accessed on 16 March 2022.
12. Steyn, L., 'SA mines plan massive power projects – but they want govt to cut red tape', *Fin24*, 23 November 2021. https://www.news24.com/fin24/companies/sa-mines-plan-massive-power-projects-but-they-want-govt-to-cut-red-tape-20211123 as accessed on 16 March 2022.
13. Atkinson, R., contrib. Sparks, A., 'Nuclear project, embezzlement linked', *Washington Post*, 31 January 1985. https://www.washingtonpost.com/archive/politics/1985/01/31/nuclear-project-embezzlement-linked/10891ea3-5eda-4ada-a3b3-6cc14c67d855/ as accessed on 16 March 2022.
14. Ibid.
15. Masondo, S., Karrim, A. and Cowan, K., 'Welcome to Babinatlou, the slush fund for greedy Eskom execs', *News24*, 4 May 2021. https://www.news24.com/news24/southafrica/investigations/eskomfiles/the-eskom-files-welcome-to-babinatlou-the-slush-fund-for-greedy-eskom-execs-20210504 as accessed on 16 March 2022.
16. Masondo, S., Karrim, A. and Cowan, K., 'Anatomy of Kusile kickbacks: How big contractors funded Eskom execs' "schools", "churches"', *News24*, 20 May 2021. https://www.news24.com/news24/southafrica/investigations/eskomfiles/the-eskom-files-anatomy-of-kusile-kickbacks-how-big-contractors-funded-eskom-execs-schools-churches-20210520 as accessed on 16 March 2022.

Chapter 2: The old hand returns
1. Author interview with Jan Oberholzer, 28 January 2022.

Chapter 3: Rome burning
1. Author interview with Jan Oberholzer, 28 January 2022.
2. Sole, S. and Brümmer, S., 'ANC front wins huge state tender', *Mail & Guardian*, 23 November 2007. https://mg.co.za/article/2007-11-23-anc-front-wins-huge-state-tender/ as accessed on 16 March 2022.
3. US Securities and Exchange Commission press release, 'SEC charges Hitachi with FCPA violations', 28 September 2015. https://www.sec.gov/news/pressrelease/2015-212.html as accessed on 16 March 2022.
4. Ibid.
5. De Lange, J., 'Modifications for Kusile and Medupi boilers', *City Press*, 24 February 2020. https://www.news24.com/citypress/business/modifications-for-kusile-and-medupi-boilers-20200222 as accessed on 17 December 2021.
6. Source documents including grievance in the author's possession.
7. Du Toit, P., Masondo, S., Karrim, A. and Cowan, K., 'Eskom crisis: SA must look at US emergency power solution, says Gordhan as diesel shortage, breakdowns worsen', *News24*, 9 November 2021. https://www.news24.com/news24/southafrica/investigations/eskom-crisis-sa-must-look-at-us-emergency

-power-solution-says-gordhan-as-diesel-shortage-breakdowns-worsen-20211108-2 as accessed on 16 March 2022.

Chapter 4: The report
1. Cowan, K., Masondo, S. and Karrim, A., 'Mystery Zondo Commission "report" may cost Eskom billions', *News24*, 16 July 2021. https://www.news24.com/news24/southafrica/investigations/eskomfiles/the-eskom-files-mystery-zondo-commission-report-may-cost-eskom-billions-20210716 as accessed on 16 March 2022.
2. Zondo Commission Report, July 2019, in the author's possession.
3. Unless otherwise specified, all quotes are from various documents, including Chettiar's grievance, the letters from Aveng, and email correspondence between Eskom and Aveng, in the author's possession.
4. Yelland, C., 'Eskom's Majuba power station rail project is a debacle', *Daily Maverick*, 31 August 2020. https://www.dailymaverick.co.za/article/2020-08-31-eskoms-majuba-power-station-rail-project-is-a-debacle/ as accessed on 16 March 2022.
5. Author's interview with anonymous Eskom source.
6. Legal opinion, claims documents and other correspondence in the author's possession.

Chapter 5: The investigation
1. Report by André de Ruyter, Eskom CEO, to the board, dated 24 August 2020. https://pmg.org.za/files/Eskom_Investigation_Report_-_COO.pdf as accessed on 16 March 2022.
2. Ngoepe, K. and Wa Afrika, M., 'Calls for Eskom to fire COO Jan Oberholzer for alleged corruption', *Sunday Independent*, 15 March 2020. https://www.iol.co.za/news/south-africa/calls-for-eskom-to-fire-coo-jan-oberholzer-for-alleged-corruption-44890297 as accessed on 16 March 2022.
3. Copy of Cassim's report in the author's possession.
4. Author interviews with anonymous Eskom sources with knowledge of the proceedings, including documents in the author's possession.
5. Smith, C., 'Eskom to investigate fire at Majuba, but at ease with coal supply delivery', *Fin24*, 18 December 2019. https://www.news24.com/fin24/economy/eskom/fire-at-majuba-power-station-extinguished-20191218 as accessed on 16 March 2022.

Chapter 6: Further investigations
1. Report by André de Ruyter, Eskom CEO, to the board, dated 24 August 2020.
2. Closing report on an investigation into allegations of failure by the Minister of Public Enterprises, Mr Pravin Gordhan, board of directors of Eskom and Eskom Holdings SOC Ltd to investigate a complaint relating to various allegations of maladministration and improper conduct against Mr Jan Oberholzer and subsequent improper application of the Protected Disclosure

Act 26 of 2000 as amended, 30 November 2021. http://www.publicprotector.org/sites/default/files/legislation_report/Closing%20Report%20Z%20Vavi%20obo%20Chettiar%20Versus%20Eskom.pdf as accessed on 4 April 2022.
3. Author interview with Jan Oberholzer, 28 January 2022.
4. Crawford Independent Associate report, dated March 2021, in author's possession.
5. Report by Jan Oberholzer, Eskom COO, dated 16 June 2021, in author's possession.
6. Chedza international website. http://www.chedza.co.za/index.php?lang=en as accessed on 16 March 2022.
7. Karrim, A., 'SIU investigating Eskom's Jan Oberholzer after 3 previous probes found no irregularities', *News24*, 10 April 2021. https://www.news24.com/news24/southafrica/investigations/siu-investigating-eskoms-jan-oberholzer-after-3-previous-probes-found-no-irregularities-20210410 as accessed on 16 March 2022.
8. Karrim, A., Cowan, K. and Masondo, S., 'Top exec Oberholzer cleared after sweeping SIU probe into claims of corruption, nepotism', *News24*, 31 August 2021. https://www.news24.com/news24/southafrica/investigations/eskomfiles/the-eskom-files-top-exec-oberholzer-cleared-after-sweeping-siu-probe-into-claims-of-corruption-nepotism-20210831 as accessed on 16 March 2022.
9. Written response from Solly Tshitangano to questions from the author, 25 March 2022.

Chapter 7: The new captain
1. Author unknown, 'EFF rejects de Ruyter's appointment as Eskom CEO', *ENCA*, 19 November 2019. https://www.enca.com/news/eff-rejects-de-ruyters-appointment-as-eskom-ceo as accessed on 17 March 2022.
2. Steyn, L. and Thompson, W., 'Inside André de Ruyter's plan to stop Eskom destroying SA', *Financial Mail*, 23 January 2020. https://www.businesslive.co.za/fm/features/cover-story/2020-01-23-inside-andr-de-ruyters-plan-to-stop-eskom-destroying-sa/ as accessed on 17 March 2022.
3. Author interview with André de Ruyter, 15 January 2022.
4. Steyn and Thompson, 'Inside André de Ruyter's plan to stop Eskom destroying SA'.
5. Author interview with André de Ruyter, 15 January 2022.

Chapter 8: The first battle
1. De Ruyter's founding affidavit in *Eskom Holdings Soc Limited* v. *Econ Oil & Energy (Pty) Ltd and Others* (21/3970), South Gauteng High Court.
2. Bowmans report of January 2019, attached to court documents.
3. Document authored by Mlonzi, obtained by Bowmans and attached to court documents.
4. Karrim, A., 'Eskom official went out of her way to help Econ Oil, and linked them up with Gigaba – probe report', *News24*, 12 April 2021. https://www.news24

.com/news24/southafrica/investigations/eskom-official-went-out-of-her-way-to-help-econ-oil-and-linked-them-up-with-gigaba-probe-report-20210412 as accessed on 17 March 2022.
5. The following information is from affidavits and other court documents in *Eskom Holdings Soc Limited* v. *Econ Oil & Energy (Pty) Ltd and Others* (21/3970).
6. De Ruyter's founding affidavit (21/3970).
7. Author interview with André de Ruyter, 15 January 2022.
8. De Ruyter's founding affidavit (21/3970).
9. Bowmans report of October 2020, attached to court documents.
10. Bowmans report of January 2019, attached to court documents.
11. Prinsloo, L. and Squazzin, A., 'Former Eskom senior manager requested Econ Oil to donate to ANC's 2014 election campaign, probe finds', *Bloomberg*, 8 April 2021. https://www.news24.com/fin24/Companies/Industrial/former-eskom-senior-manager-requested-econ-oil-to-fund-ancs-2014-election-campaign-probe-finds-20210408 as accessed on 4 April 2022.
12. Answering affidavit by Nothemba Mlonzi, 12 February 2021, Gauteng High Court, Johannesburg, case number 3970/21, *Eskom Holdings Soc Ltd* v. *Econ Oil & Energy and Others*.
13. Answering affidavit by Nothemba Mlonzi, 19 April 2021, ibid.
14. Ibid.
15. Appeal Hearing Decision, *Jerome Mthembu* v. *News24*, 24 November 2021. https://presscouncil.org.za/Ruling/View/appeal-hearing-decision-jerome-mthembu-vs-news24-4594 as accessed on 4 April 2022.
16. Answering affidavit by Nothemba Mlonzi, 19 April 2021.
17. Copy of letter authored by Mlonzi, attached to court documents.
18. Email from Dabengwa, attached to court documents.
19. Contained in court documents.
20. Minutes of Eskom board meeting, 25 March 2020.
21. André de Ruyter's submission to the board, dated 28 May 2020.
22. Author interview with André de Ruyter, 15 January 2022.
23. De Ruyter's submission to the board, dated 28 May 2020.
24. Author interview with André de Ruyter, 15 January 2022.
25. Dabengwa's letter to the board, dated 8 June 2020.
26. Report by Advocate Wim Trengove to Eskom, 14 July 2020.
27. Makinana, A., 'Eskom board member resigns over "fundamental differences of principle"', *TimesLIVE*, 27 July 2020. https://www.timeslive.co.za/news/south-africa/2020-07-27-eskom-board-member-resigns-over-fundamental-differences-of-principle/ as accessed on 17 March 2022.

Chapter 9: 'You're just bullshitting'

1. Author interview with Sifiso Dabengwa, 12 February 2022.
2. Description of board submission in court documents, *Eskom Holdings Soc Limited* v. *Econ Oil & Energy (Pty) Ltd and Others* (21/3970).
3. André de Ruyter's submission to the board, dated 28 May 2020.

NOTES

4. Ibid.
5. Ibid.
6. Author interview with Sifiso Dabengwa, 12 February 2022.
7. De Ruyter's submission to the board, dated 28 May 2020.
8. Answering affidavit by Nothemba Mlonzi, 19 April 2021.
9. Ibid.
10. Author interview with Sifiso Dabengwa, 12 February 2022.

Chapter 10: The second battle

1. Author interview with André de Ruyter, 15 January 2022.
2. Sguazzin, A. and Prinsloo, L., 'Eskom to cancel contract after probe', *BusinessLIVE*, 31 July 2020. https://www.businesslive.co.za/bd/national/2020-07-31-eskom-to-cancel-contract-after-probe/ as accessed on 17 March 2022.
3. Makwakwa, T., 'No progress in criminal case laid over a year ago against Eskom CEO André de Ruyter', *Daily News*, 18 November 2021. https://www.iol.co.za/dailynews/news/no-progress-in-criminal-case-laid-over-a-year-ago-against-eskom-ceo-andre-de-ruyter-459e3c95-a3bf-456d-84a2-d8ae334cfc8b as accessed on 17 March 2022.
4. Hlongwane, S., 'Limpopo textbook crisis: whistleblower out in the cold', *Daily Maverick*, 19 July 2012. https://www.dailymaverick.co.za/article/2012-07-19-limpopo-textbook-crisis-whistleblower-out-in-the-cold/ as accessed on 18 March 2022.
5. Documents including emails in the author's possession, as well as interviews with anonymous Eskom sources during the course of 2021.
6. Shange, N., 'Eskom contractor ABB agrees to pay back R1.6bn for "over-payments"', *TimesLIVE*, 11 December 2020. https://www.timeslive.co.za/news/south-africa/2020-12-11-eskom-contractor-abb-agrees-to-pay-back-r16bn-for-over-payments/ as accessed on 17 March 2022.
7. Written response from Solly Tshitangano to questions from the author, 25 March 2022.
8. Author interview with André de Ruyter, 15 January 2022.
9. Cowan, K., 'Solly Tshitangano claims Bowmans probe at Eskom is unlawful ... but he approved it', *News24*, 5 June 2021. https://www.news24.com/news24/southafrica/investigations/eskomfiles/the-eskom-files-solly-tshitangano-claims-bowmans-probe-at-eskom-is-unlawful-but-he-approved-it-20210605 as accessed on 17 March 2022.
10. Letter from the SIU to Eskom in the author's possession.
11. Written response from Solly Tshitangano to questions from the author, 25 March 2022.
12. Letter in the author's possession.
13. Written response from Solly Tshitangano to questions from the author, 25 March 2022.
14. Masondo, S. and Cowan, K., 'Respected but suspended: Eskom's Solly Tshitangano faced similar misconduct charges in 2005', *News24*, 10 April 2021.

https://www.news24.com/news24/southafrica/investigations/respected-but-sus pended-solly-tshitangano-faced-similar-charges-to-eskom-complaints-in-2005 -20210410 as accessed on 17 March 2022.
15. Cowan, K., Masondo, S., Karrim, A. and Du Toit, P., 'Axed Eskom boss Solly Tshitangano was "intent on promoting the interests of Econ Oil"', *News24*, 29 May 2021. https://www.news24.com/news24/southafrica/investigations/ eskomfiles/in-full-axed-eskom-boss-solly-tshitangano-was-intent-on-promoting -the-interests-of-econ-oil-20210529 as accessed on 18 March 2022.

Chapter 11: The allegations of racism

1. Cowan, K. and Masondo, S., 'The 22 charges against suspended Eskom procurement chief Solly Tshitangano', *News24*, 9 April 2021. https://www.news24.com/ news24/southafrica/investigations/in-detail-the-22-charges-against-suspended -eskom-procurement-chief-solly-tshitangano-20210408 as accessed on 17 March 2022.
2. Copy of De Ruyter's affidavit in the author's possession.
3. Omarjee, L., 'Scopa halts probe into claims of racism and abuse of power against Eskom's De Ruyter', *News24*, 7 April 2021. https://www.news24.com/fin24/ Companies/Industrial/scopa-halts-probe-into-claims-of-racism-and-abuse-of -power-against-eskoms-de-ruyter-20210407 as accessed on 17 March 2022.
4. Copy of Cassim's report, dated 28 May 2021, attached to court documents.
5. Written response from Solly Tshitangano to questions posed by the author, 25 March 2022.
6. Copy of Semenya's report, dated 1 June 2021, attached to court documents.
7. Written response from Solly Tshitangano to questions posed by the author, 25 March 2022.
8. Author interview with André de Ruyter, 15 January 2022.

Chapter 12: Smelling a rat

1. Tsekoa, K., 'An analysis of challenges in implementing an equipment reliability improvement strategy: Case study Eskom Camden Power Station', Master of Technology Management research report, University of Pretoria, 31 July 2017. https://repository.up.ac.za/bitstream/handle/2263/ 62797/Tsekoa_Analysis_2017.pdf?sequence=1&isAllowed=y as accessed on 28 March 2022.
2. Cui, R.Y., Hultman, N., Edwards, M.R., et al., 'Quantifying operational lifetimes for coal power plants under the Paris goals', *Nature Communications* 10 (4759), 2019. https://doi.org/10.1038/s41467-019-12618-3 as accessed on 28 March 2022.
3. Author unknown, '"Keep the lights on" policy unsustainable, says Eskom', *ENCA*, 23 February 2015. https://www.enca.com/south-africa/eskoms-keep -lights-policy-contributing-bad-air-quality as accessed on 28 March 2022.
4. Cowan, K., 'Glossary of terms to assist understanding of Eskom key performance indicators', *News24*, 25 October 2021. https://www.news24.com/

news24/southafrica/investigations/eskomfiles/glossary-of-terms-to-assist-understanding-of-eskom-key-performance-indicators-20211024 as accessed on 28 March 2022.
5. Author interview with anonymous senior Eskom source.
6. All EAF data provided to the author by Eskom.
7. Cowan, K., Karrim, A. and Masondo, S., 'Driven to destruction: How Eskom power stations were "run into the ground"', *News24*, 29 October 2021. https://www.news24.com/news24/southafrica/investigations/eskomfiles/the-eskom-files-driven-to-destruction-how-eskom-power-stations-were-run-into-the-ground-20211028 as accessed on 28 March 2022.
8. Document in the author's possession.
9. Ibid.
10. Cowan, K., Karrim, A. and Masondo, S., 'Over the brink: Data shows how Koko's Eskom seemingly cooked the electricity books', *News24*, 25 October 2021. https://www.news24.com/news24/southafrica/investigations/eskomfiles/the-eskom-files-over-the-brink-data-shows-how-kokos-eskom-seemingly-cooked-the-electricity-books-20211025 as accessed on 28 March 2022.
11. Author interview with anonymous senior Eskom source.
12. Practice note shared with the author by Matshela Koko.
13. Koko, M., 'Responses by Matshela Koko to questions from News24', *News24*, 25 October 2021. https://www.news24.com/news24/southafrica/investigations/eskomfiles/responses-by-matshela-koko-to-questions-from-news24-20211024 as accessed on 28 March 2022.
14. Author interview with anonymous senior Eskom source.
15. Koko, 'Responses by Matshela Koko to questions from News24'.
16. Cowan, Karrim and Masondo, 'Driven to destruction: How Eskom power stations were "run into the ground"'.
17. Koko, 'Responses by Matshela Koko to questions from News24'.
18. Eskom data provided to the author.
19. Ibid.
20. https://twitter.com/koko_matshela/status/1097466097991933953 as accessed on 4 April 2022.
21. https://twitter.com/koko_matshela/status/1097469424347557889 as accessed on 4 April 2022.
22. Author interview with anonymous senior Eskom official.
23. Eskom 2021 Annual Report.
24. 'Corrective statement on Koko following Press Council appeals ruling', *News24*, 12 April 2022. https://www.news24.com/news24/southafrica/investigations/corrective-statement-on-koko-following-press-council-appeals-ruling-20220412 as accessed on 21 April 2022.
25. See Eberhard, A., 'SA still needs Eskom but also new generation capacity'. *Business Day*, 21 April 2022. https://www.businesslive.co.za/bd/opinion/2022-04-21-anton-eberhard-sa-still-needs-eskom-but-also-new-generation-capacity/ as accessed on 4 May 2022.

Chapter 13: 'We would like you to look after this place'

1. Masweneng. K., '"Andre De Ruyter must fall": Black Business Council calls for Eskom boss's head', *TimesLIVE*, 8 November 2021. https://www.timeslive.co.za/news/south-africa/2021-11-08-andre-de-ruyter-must-fall-black-business-council-calls-for-eskom-bosss-head/ as accessed on 22 March 2022.
2. Author interview with Professor Malegapuru Makgoba, 17 February 2022.
3. National Orders profile of M.W. Makgoba on https://www.thepresidency.gov.za/national-orders/recipient/professor-malegapuru-william-makgoba as accessed on 22 March 2022.
4. Makgoba, M.W., 'Life Esidimeni and the ghosts of our past: "It's time to decolonise our ethics"', *Mail & Guardian*, 16 August 2018. https://mg.co.za/article/2018-08-16-00-lifeesidimeni-and-the-ghosts-of-our-past-its-time-to-decolonise-our-ethics/ as accessed on 22 March 2022.
5. Geber, J., 'Businessman Jabu Mabuza to chair Eskom, Koko and Singh to be removed immediately', *News24*, 20 January 2018. https://www.news24.com/Fin24/breaking-new-eskom-chair-announced-20180120 as accessed on 22 March 2022.
6. Author interview with Professor Malegapuru Makgoba, 17 February 2022.
7. SIU presentation to SCOPA, 17 February 2021.
8. Author interview with Professor Malegapuru Makgoba, 17 February 2022.

Chapter 14: 'Did I mention the debt?'

1. Author interview with André de Ruyter, 15 January 2022.
2. Author interview with Jan Oberholzer, 26 January 2022.
3. Author interview with anonymous Eskom official.
4. Du Toit, P., 'R131bn from rich countries will help Eskom speed up new power projects, De Ruyter says', *Fin24*, 3 November 2021. https://www.news24.com/fin24/economy/r131bn-from-rich-countries-will-help-eskom-speed-up-new-power-projects-de-ruyter-says-20211103 as accessed on 17 March 2022.
5. Mkentane, L., 'Mantashe puts coal before just energy transition', *Business Day*, 13 January 2022. https://www.businesslive.co.za/bd/national/2022-01-13-mantashe-puts-coal-before-just-energy-transition/ as accessed on 17 March 2022.
6. Ibid.
7. Author interview with anonymous energy sector insider.
8. Author unknown, 'Soot, loot, reboot', *The Economist*, 22 January 2022. https://www.economist.com/middle-east-and-africa/2022/01/22/south-africa-the-worlds-coal-junkie-tries-to-quit as accessed on 17 March 2022.
9. Author interview with anonymous energy sector insider.

Epilogue

1. Author interview with André de Ruyter, 15 January 2022.
2. Author interview with Jan Oberholzer, 26 January 2022.
3. Author interview with Professor Malegapuru Makgoba, 17 February 2022.

Additional references

Blackout: The Eskom Crisis by James-Brent Styan (Jonathan Ball, 2015), a meticulous account of the decline of Eskom, the political interference and how load shedding came to be. Highly recommended for anyone wanting to understand Eskom.

The Eskom Files, a News24 investigation during the course of 2021, available at www.news24.com/news24/southafrica/investigations/eskomfiles. The work details the collapse of governance, corruption and largesse at Kusile Power Station and is well worth reading to understand the consequences of pervasive graft.

Eskom Annual Reports – Eskom's website, www.eskom.co.za, has a complete archive of annual reports from 1925 onwards. Reading the summaries from the chairperson and chief executive over the past five decades provides fascinating insight into the metamorphosis of the utility, from best to broken.

Judicial Commission of Inquiry into State Capture report, Volume Four.

Licence to Loot: How the Plunder of Eskom and Other Parastatals Almost Sank South Africa by Stephan Hofstatter (Penguin Books, 2018), an account of the state capture years at Eskom. It is essential reading for a greater understanding of the challenges faced and created by state capture at the power utility.

Official historical accounts on Eskom's Heritage web page, available at https://www.eskom.co.za/sites/heritage/Pages/History-in-Decades.aspx.

The O'Malley Archives, a painstaking history of the ANC by Padraig O'Malley, particularly subsections 'The Sabotage Campaign' and 'List of MK Operations', available at https://omalley.nelsonmandela.org/omalley/index.php/site/q/03lv02424/04lv02730/05lv02918/06lv02946.htm.

'The Pricing of Electricity in South Africa: A Critical Assessment of the De Villiers Commission of Inquiry', Brian Kantor, *Managerial and Decision Economics*, vol. 9, no. 4, Wiley, 1988, pp. 301–09, available at http://www.jstor.org/stable/2487521.

Index

ABB 131, 145
affirmative action 146
African National Congress
   see ANC
Afrikaans language 87
air compressors 163–164
Alstom 40, 44
analyst community 94
ANC 21, 37–40, 103, 123, 193
Ankerlig Power Station 16,
   35–36, 151
Ankerlig Transmission
   Koeberg Second Supply
   Project *see* ATKSS
apartheid 10
Arnot Power Station 73
ash dam at Camden Power
   Station 62
ATKSS 47
attacks on De Ruyter and
   Oberholzer, impact of
   7, 11, 44–47, 185–187,
   194–195
Attard Montalto, Peter 83
autism 32–33
automatic shutdowns 163
Aveng 47, 49–50, 52–62, 66,
   69, 71–72
Avon peaking power plant
   169

Babinatlou Business Services
   25
Basil Read 70
Baxter, Roger 22
Beeld 13

Bhowani, Ishan 156–160,
   164–168
BKS 84, 85
Black & Veatch 46, 64, 69,
   72–80
Bloomberg 103
board of Eskom 24, 185
boilers 8, 38–39, 44, 149, 153
Boston Consulting Group
   102
Botha, Hannes 91
Botha, Johan 91
Bowmans 25–26, 44, 65, 71,
   75, 102–108, 111–114,
   118–123, 129–134
BP 120, 121, 135
breakdowns 9–10, 155–161,
   165, 168, 171, 173
Brown, Lynne 176
Bruinette Kruger Stoffberg
   see BKS
Brümmer, Stefaans 38
Bud Group 109
Business Day 190

Camden Power Station 62,
   73
capacity shortages 14–19,
   36–37, 151, 168–170
capital expansion
   programme 15–16, 30,
   73, 76
card system 20–21, 157–158,
   162–164, 166, 168, 171
Cassim, Calib 137, 177
Cassim, Nazeer 47, 64–66,
   69, 137–138, 142–143,
   181–182
CCMA 63–64
CCTV cameras 7
CEO position at Eskom
   3–4, 186–187
Chancellor House 37–40
Chase Manhattan Bank 23
Chedza International Loss
   Adjusters 79
Chettiar, Mark 47, 49–51,
   55–66, 69, 71–72, 80
chief executive officer
   position at Eskom 3–4,
   186–187
Child, Dennis 46
China 90
Cloete, Chris 87
coal 2, 19, 51–52, 58, 149,
   153, 188–191
coal mills 153
cold reserve 160–162, 164,
   166–168
Coleman, Elsie 138
collieries 51
Commission for
   Conciliation,
   Mediation and
   Arbitration *see* CCMA
compensation events 54
compressors 163–164
Condea 90, 93
conflicts of interest 79–80
Constable, David 92
cooling systems 152
COP26 188, 190

corruption 4–5, 11, 14, 22–26, 37–45, 50, 75, 176–177
Corruption Watch 63–64
Covid-19 pandemic 3
CR17 campaign 79
Crawford Independent Associate 46, 74–81
Crawford, Russell 70
Crompton, Rod 89

Dabengwa, Sifiso 79–80, 100–102, 110–117, 121–126, 135, 181–182
Daily Maverick 11
Daily News 129
Dames, Brian 3–4, 40–41
Davies, Pat 89, 91
Davis, Sir Mick 18
debt of Eskom 16, 21, 52, 188
Dedisa peaking power plant 169
defamation 127–129
demand *see* electricity demand
De Ruyter, André
  attacks on 4, 6–7, 11, 84, 175, 177, 185, 187
  as CEO 3–5, 7, 83–84, 95, 186–188
  in China 90
  civil suit 128–129
  criminal defamation 127–129
  on debt 188
  Econ Oil 97–102, 107–108, 110–115, 117–122, 126
  family of 84–86, 90
  in Germany 90–92
  on hope 194–195
  Kusile Power Station 39
  Makgoba on 178–183
  in Mozambique 89
  at Nampak 83, 92–95, 146

Oberholzer and 47, 50, 69–72
  on procurement policies 14, 132–133, 145
  racism, accusations of 6, 11, 83, 90, 101, 139, 141–147
  on renewable energy 191
  on sabotage 2–3, 6, 12
  at Sasol 86–93
  studies of 85–86, 88–89
  at Tolplan 85, 86
  on travelling 86–88
  Tshitangano and 83–84, 137–139, 143–147, 185
  youth of 84–86
De Villiers' Commission 17
diesel 16, 99, 156
Directorate for Priority Crime Investigation *see* Hawks
disciplinary card system *see* card system
Dladla, Johnny 4
Doolaard, A. den 86
drones 7
Dukashe, Phillip 10, 46
Du Preez, Alida 30
Du Toit, Pieter 158, 172
Duvha Power Station 29, 73

EAF 151–158, 161–163, 165–168
Econ Oil 97–132, 134–137, 139, 141–143, 145, 147, 181–182
Economic Freedom Fighters *see* EFF
economic growth 13, 17, 170, 193–194
Economist, The 94, 190–191
EduSolutions 130
EFF 83, 187, 191
electricity demand 1–2, 13–14, 18

electrification programmes 18, 30–32, 151
employees of Eskom 24, 146, 176–177
energy availability factor *see* EAF
energy utilisation factor *see* EUF
Engen 120–121
Engineering Houses Panel 72–73
ENSafrica 60
ESBI 39, 72–73, 78
Eskom Enterprises 34, 40
'Eskom Files' 26, 61, 158
Esor Construction 25
Etzinger, Andrew 45–46
EUF 154–156, 166–167
evening peak 1–2
Exco Tender Committee 134, 136–137

Faku, Mkhuseli 109
FFS 99, 103, 109, 111, 118, 137
FIFA World Cup (2010) 151
Fin24 188
Financial Mail 83, 92
financing organisations, international 21
fires 8–9, 67
Flanagan, Sean 56–58
fossil-fuel projects 21
free-text procurement 132–133
Fuel Firing Systems (FFS) Refiners *see* FFS
fuel oil 97–98
  see also Econ Oil
Fullerton, Glenn 93

Gcabashe, Thulani 4, 35
General Electric 44, 47
generation load factor *see* GLF
Gigaba, Malusi 98, 106
GLF 154, 156, 166–167

INDEX

Global Initiative against Transnational Organized Crime 26, 158
Gordhan, Pravin 5, 6, 8, 24–25, 47, 69, 83, 142, 145, 180
Gourikwa Power Station 16, 35–36, 151
Grootvlei Power Station 73, 162
group capital division 35, 49–50
Group Five 47
Gumede, Nhlanhla 89
Gupta family 4, 23–24

Hadebe, Phakamani 4–5, 20, 24, 42, 170
Hawks 3, 12
Hendrina Power Station 134, 162
Hewu, Bartlett 49, 60, 70
Hitachi 37–40, 44
Hlakudi, France 23, 25
hydrogen leaks 163

IFC 97, 100–101, 110, 134
independent power producers *see* IPPs
industrialisation 189
'infant mortality period' 149–150
Ingula pumped storage scheme 6, 15–16, 36–37, 73, 151, 160, 168–169
integrated resource plan *see* IRP
interim payment certificates *see* IPCs
international financing organisations 21
investment and finance committee *see* IFC
investment community 94

investor confidence 14
IPCs 55
IPPs 14, 19–21, 35, 160, 168–170, 190
IRP 19, 190

Japan 87
job creation 19, 192
Judicial Commission of Inquiry into Allegations of State Capture, Corruption and Fraud in the Public Sector *see* Zondo Commission
just energy transition 190

Kardol, Bas 88
Karrim, Azarrah 163
Katz, Michael 113–114, 125
'keep the lights on' policy 151
Kendal Power Station 18
key performance indicators (for power stations) 151–170
Kganyago, Kaizer 80
Kgomoeswana, Hudson 23, 25
Khoza, Zethembe 4
Khumalo, Themba 60
kickback schemes 23, 25
Koeberg nuclear power station 7, 10, 17, 22, 47, 154
Koko, Matshela 4, 5, 19–21, 107, 151, 155–173
Komati Power Station 73, 162
Korea 87
Kriel Power Station 73, 157, 162, 165–168
Kusile Power Station
 Black & Veatch contract 46, 72
 boilers 38–40
 Bowmans 25–26, 44, 65, 75

 costs 37, 44
 new capacity 6, 15–16, 36–37, 150–151, 160, 168–169

law enforcement 11–12
'legacy' coal stations 150, 151, 154–156, 160–161, 168
legal costs 49, 66
Lekwe power station (planned) 18
Le Riche, John 70
Lethabo Power Station 1–3, 6–7, 12, 18
Leven van een landloper, Het 86
Life Esidimeni tragedy 176
lifespan of power generation units 149–150
lifestyle audits 70
limpet mines 10
load shedding 2–8, 14, 17, 20–21, 24, 151, 156, 168–170, 173, 195
Lomas, Michael 23, 25
long-term contract placements 145
Loots, Johan 98

Mabuza, David 8
Mabuza, Jabu 4–5, 24, 49, 60, 63–65, 70, 132, 176
Madonsela, Thuli 24
Magubane, Nelisiwe 89
Mahanyele, Mohale 79
Mahanyele, Mpho 79–80
Mahanyele, Phuthi 79–80
Maharaj, Avin 70
Mahlangu, Jabu 49
Mail & Guardian 38
maintenance
 deferred 6, 18, 42
 'festival' (2015) 160
 'keep the lights on' policy 151

215

opportunity 161
planned 150–152, 155–156, 161, 165–167, 171, 173
unplanned 156–157, 159, 166
Majuba Colliery 51
Majuba Power Station 9, 16, 18, 51, 151, 154–155
Majuba rail project 9, 47, 49–62, 67
Makgoba, Malegapuru 5, 11, 110–113, 115, 138–139, 144, 175–184, 194–195
Makwana, Mpho 4
Mantashe, Gwede 8, 19, 21, 189–191
Marah, Thandi 98, 102–109, 111–112, 117–120, 122–123, 129
Maritz, Sean 4
Maroga, Jacob 3, 40
Marshall, Andrew 93
Masango, Abram 23, 25, 50
Massey, Ian 54, 57–58
Matimba Power Station 18
Matjila, Collin 4
Matla Power Station 73
Matona, Tshediso 4
Mavimbela, Jabulane 44–46
Mbeki, Thabo 15, 17–18
Mboweni, Tito 94–95
McKinsey 102, 108, 114, 119–122
McRae, Ian 4, 18, 194
media coverage 11, 127–129, 187
Medupi Power Station 6–7, 15–16, 36–40, 44, 65, 72, 150–151, 160, 163, 168–169
meritocracy 179–180
middlemen 44
mills *see* coal mills
mining sector 19, 21–22
Mitsubishi 44
Mkhawane, Eric 63

Mkhwebane, Busisiwe 72
Mlonzi, Nothemba 97–99, 102–109, 118, 123–124, 127–129, 135–136
Molefe, Brian 4, 5, 20, 168
Möller, Danie 49, 50–51, 55, 57–62, 66
Molokwane, Pulane 111–112
Mongalo, Tshepo 112
monopoly on electricity generation 19, 22
Moosajee, Aslam 128
Moosa, Valli 38
Morgan, Allen 4
morning peak 2
Mosala, Itumeleng 61
Mouton, Werner 110, 138, 144–145
Mthembu, Jerome 70, 107, 131–133
Murray & Roberts 72–73, 78

Nampak, De Ruyter at 83, 92–95, 146
National Prosecuting Authority 9, 12, 176
'national service' 7, 187
National Transmission Company 181, 188
National Treasury 9, 119, 130–131
National Union of Mineworkers *see* NUM
News24
  Bowmans report 103–104, 107
  'Eskom Files' 26, 61
  Koko's tenure as CEO 20–21, 158, 162–163, 170–172
  Majuba Power Station 8
  Majuba rail project 61, 67
  SIU 80
  on Tshitangano 132, 138

Ngoepe, Bernard 107, 171–172
Nombembe, Terence 49
Nova Economics study 170
nuclear power 20, 154
NUM 8, 83, 191
Nxumalo, Bheki 46
Nyenrode Business University, Netherlands 88–89

O&S 90–92, 93
Oberholzer, Anna 27
Oberholzer, Jacobus 27
Oberholzer, Jan
  attacks on 4, 7, 11, 44–47, 63, 66–67, 80–81, 175, 177, 182, 185, 187
  Black & Veatch contract 64, 72–79
  Bowmans 44, 65
  as business owner 41
  Camden Power Station 62
  Cassim report 64–66
  as COO 25, 41–45
  EAF 156
  Econ Oil 137
  electrification programme 30–32
  at Eskom 27, 29–34
  family of 27–28, 32–33
  on hope 194
  lifestyle audit 70
  Majuba rail project 54–58, 60–61, 71–72
  on new capacity 15–16, 35–37, 39
  resignation from Eskom 39–41
  retirement of 186
  on sabotage 7, 9
  schedule of 32
  SIU 80–81
  at Stefanutti Stocks 41
  Stefanutti Stocks shares 63–65, 69–71

INDEX

at Technology Services International 34–35
youth of 27–29
Zondo Commission report 49–51
Oberholzer, Lindy 29–30, 32–33, 41, 80
OCLF 152, 167
O'Connor, Peter 35
Oosdraai coal-export plant 86
open cycle gas turbines 35–36, 73, 151, 154, 156, 169
operating excursions (running units after stoppage is needed) 14, 20–21, 24, 164
opportunity maintenance 161
organisational culture 195
other capability loss factor *see* OCLF
outages 157–158, 167

Parsons Brinckerhoff Power Africa *see* PB Power Africa
partial load losses 153, 157, 160, 164
PB Power Africa 72, 78
PCLF 152, 167
peaking power plants (peakers) 169
performance incentive scheme 157–158, 162
performance indicators for power stations *see* key performance indicators
performance of staff 146
PFMA 75, 164
planned capability loss factor *see* PCLF
planned maintenance 150–152, 155–156, 161, 165–167, 171, 173

police *see* South African Police Service
policy and regulatory challenges 14, 150–151, 189–192
pollution 13, 188
power generation units 149–151
power purchase agreements 19, 169–170
power station managers 20–21, 157–158, 162–164
power stations, new 14–19, 36–37, 151, 168–170
press coverage 11, 127–129, 187
Press Ombud 107, 171
privatisation 21
procurement policies 14, 44, 52, 132–133
protection systems 163
public demands 180
Public Finance Management Act *see* PFMA
Public Protector 24, 47, 72
Pule, Elsie 137
pylons 1–3

racism, accusations of
  against author 171–172
  against De Ruyter 6, 11, 83, 90, 101, 139, 141–147
  Makgoba on 179–181
  against Oberholzer 11, 45–46
  against Zulu 109
Rademeyer, Gert 22–23
rail project *see* Majuba rail project
Ramaphosa, Cyril 5, 6, 8, 21, 24, 79, 176–177, 180
Ramolefe, Khotso 45–46

regulatory challenges *see* policy and regulatory challenges
remuneration 186
renewable energy 19–20, 22, 39, 190–191
retention monies 54–56
Ria Tenda Trust 79
road transport 9, 52, 58
running units after stoppage is needed *see* operating excursions

sabotage 1–3, 5–12, 67
SAFTU 63–64, 69, 72
Sasol 11, 98, 105, 117–118, 120–121, 135, 137
Sasol, De Ruyter at 86–92, 93
Sasol Olefins and Surfactants *see* O&S
Scheppers, Segomoco 9
Schutte, Chris 45
SCOPA 74, 141–143
SEC (Securities and Exchange Commission) 38
self-generation allowance 21–22
Semenya, Ishmael 142–146
sensors 8, 163–164
Sere wind farm 39, 73
Shivambu, Floyd 191
shutdowns, automatic 163
Singh, Anoj 5
Singh, Binesh 70
SIU 24, 47, 71, 80–81, 132–134, 176
skills shortages 16, 24, 37, 39, 75, 101, 195
smelters 21
SNG Grant Thornton 159
social media 171–172, 187
Sole, Sam 38
South African Federation of Trade Unions *see* SAFTU

217

South African Police Service 12, 86, 127–128
spares 43, 95
Special Investigating Unit *see* SIU
sponsorships 102–103, 123
staff of Eskom 24, 146, 176–177
Standing Committee on Public Accounts *see* SCOPA
state capture 4–5, 23–24
State Security Agency 12
steam leaks 163
Stefanutti Stocks 25, 41, 44, 47, 63–65, 69–71
Stephen, Rob 31
STERF committee 164
Steyn, Grové 17
Stock, Grant 53–55
Sunday Express 23
Sunday Independent 63–64
systemic approach 177–178
system operators 153

tariffs 188–189
technical expertise *see* skills shortages
Technology Services International 35
temperature sensors 163–164
Tenova Mining & Minerals 25, 57
theft 45
tied collieries 51
TimesLIVE 116
tipplers 52, 54, 57
Tolplan 85, 86
trade unions *see* unions
transformation 105–106
transmission 42, 188

transparency 159
Transvaler, Die 10
Treasury *see* National Treasury
Trengove, Wim 115–116, 121, 124–125, 181
Trindade, Antonio 23, 25
trucks *see* road transport
Tshitangano, Mmbulahiseni Solomon (Solly)
  background of 130–132, 138–139
  Bowmans 131–134
  De Ruyter and 83–84, 137–139, 143–147, 185
  disciplinary hearing of 142–143
  Econ Oil 101, 107, 119–121, 130, 134–137, 141
  Kusile Power Station 70
  Oberholzer and 74, 78, 81
  suspended 141
Tubular Construction Projects 23, 25, 44, 50
turbines 44, 149
Turner, Rob 87–88
Tutuka Power Station 8–9, 11–12, 18, 45, 95, 162
Twitter 171–172, 187

UCLF 152–153, 155, 167–168
Umkhonto we Sizwe 10, 11
unbundling of Eskom 181, 188, 195
unions 21, 83, 191
United Nations Climate Change Conference *see* COP26
units *see* power generation units

unplanned breakdowns 9–10, 155–161, 165, 168, 171, 173
unplanned capability loss factor *see* UCLF
unplanned losses 162, 165–166, 168, 173
unplanned maintenance 156–157, 159, 166
US Securities and Exchange Commission *see* SEC

vacuum losses 153
valves controlling water supply 8–9, 67
vandalism 8, 9
Van der Bijl, Hendrik 189
Van der Spuy, Clive 128
Van der Walt, Chris 29
Vavi, Zwelinzima 64

water quality 149
whistleblowers 63–65, 71–72, 118, 130, 147
white males, criticism of hiring of 175, 180–181
Wilkinson, Rodney 10–11
wind farms 39, 73
working capital 95
World Bank 52

Yelland, Chris 51–52

Zambia 41
Zondo Commission 5, 24, 47, 49–51, 58, 60–62, 65–66, 71
Zondo, Raymond 5, 61
Zulu, Ntuthuko 108–109, 124
Zuma, Jacob 4, 5, 15, 24, 176